DARK NIGHT
OF SOUL
THE

DARK NIGHT
OF
THE SOUL

AND OTHER GREAT WORKS

BY

SAINT JOHN
OF THE CROSS

BRIDGE
LOGOS
FOUNDATION

Alachua, Florida 32615

The material within this book has been adapted from the works of several translators.

Bridge-Logos
Alachua, FL 32615 USA

Dark Night of the Soul
by Saint John of the Cross

Rewritten and updated by Lloyd B. Hildebrand

Printed in the United States of America.

Library of Congress Catalog Card Number: 2007929857
International Standard Book Number: 978-0-88270-402-9

Scripture quotations are from the *King James Version* of the Bible.

G163.317.B.m1003.35220

CONTENTS

BOOK I THE DARK NIGHT OF THE SENSES

BOOK II THE DARK NIGHT OF THE SPIRIT

FOREWORD

That the trial of your faith, being much more precious
than of gold that perisheth, though it be tried with fire,
might be found unto praise and honour and glory at the
appearing of Jesus Christ: whom having not seen, ye love;
in whom, though now ye see him not, yet believing,
ye rejoice with joy unspeakable and full of glory:
receiving the end of your faith,
even the salvation of your souls
(1 Peter 1:7-9).

After working so closely with the poignant writings and inspiring life of Saint John of the Cross, I must say that I have learned to truly love him, for, through his writings, he still is a vessel of God's love to the world, a fully dedicated servant of Jesus Christ. His personal goal was to find union with God through love, and I'm sure he attained that goal as a result of the experiences he had to endure during his own personal "dark night of the soul," which he describes so vividly and compellingly through both poetry and prose. His perseverance in doing so serves as a great model for us all.

Like the ancient Israelites, Saint John of the Cross learned that times of wandering in the dry wilderness of the desert are actually good for the soul. In such dark and arid times one learns to realize what is truly important in life and one is purged from all impediments and hindrances that keep him or her away from deep intimacy with God. It was during his own "dark night of the soul"—the trial as by fire—that he learned how to detach from the world and the self-life. And like Christ, during His time in the wilderness, Saint John also learned how to overcome the temptations of the evil one.

There are some similarities between *Dark Night of the Soul* and other great Christian classics, such as the writings of Madame Jeanne Guyon, Saint Augustine, Thomas à Kempis, Fenélon, Brother Lawrence, Saint Bernard of Clairvaux, and John Bunyan. In fact, the struggles and tribulations that are faced by the soul in *Dark Night of the Soul* are quite comparable to what Christian went through in Bunyan's *Pilgrim's Progress*, and what Virgil faced in Dante's *The Divine Comedy*. In the latter work, human reason could take Virgil only so far in his quest for union with God; it was divine love, of which Saint John of the Cross writes so eloquently, that finally allowed Virgil to enter Paradise.

Paradise is the place where one finds union with God. It is the Promised Land, the Kingdom of God, the City of God, and the Kingdom of Heaven. It is where God's throne is located and the place where the angels praise the Father in their celestial choirs. It is the true home of all those who spend their lives seeking the face of God, as did Saint John of the Cross.

This glorious place is described in the Book of the Revelation as follows: "And he shewed me a pure river of water of life, clear as crystal, proceeding out of the throne of God and of the Lamb. In the midst of the street of it, and on either side of the river, was there the tree of life, which bare twelve manner of fruits, and yielded her fruit every month: and the leaves of the tree were for the healing of the nations. And there shall be no more curse: but the throne of God and of the Lamb shall be in it; and his servants shall serve him: and they shall see his face; and his name shall be in their foreheads. And there shall be no night there; and they need no candle, neither light of the sun; for the Lord

God giveth them light: and they shall reign for ever and ever" (Revelation 22:1–5).

As the soul emerges from the dark night it has had to endure, a brilliant light awaits it, and the properties of this light include cleansing, purity, renewed vision, spiritual understanding, deep wisdom, and the warmth of union with God's love. This is what Saint John of the Cross was seeking, and it is what he ultimately found. In this sense he represents every one of us who wants to experience the fullness of God's glory and leave the ways of the world behind. The Apostle Paul wrote: "Giving thanks unto the Father, which hath made us meet to be partakers of the inheritance of the saints in light: who hath delivered us from the power of darkness, and hath translated us into the kingdom of his dear Son" (Colossians 1:12–13). As you read *Love's Living Flame*, and *Dark Night of the Soul*, you will experience this same spiritual deliverance and be translated into the Kingdom of the Son of God—a glorious kingdom of light and love.

Furthermore, you will learn vital spiritual truths from this extraordinary teacher, priest, poet, philosopher, prophet, mystic, spiritual pioneer, and writer; and he will lead you through your own "dark night of the soul." All the way along he will be your guide, showing you that the pathway you take is paved with faith, hope, and love. (See 1 Corinthians 13:13.) Ultimately, like him, you will find the radiant and glorious light that awaits you—the "living flame of love"—that will take you the rest of the way into the Kingdom of God, where you will enjoy wonderful intimacy and union with God your heavenly Father, and your Savior, the Lord Jesus Christ. You will hear the Holy Spirit speaking to you through these pages, and you will be changed forever.

For Saint John of the Cross this amazing spiritual pilgrimage began when he was a boy in Fontiveros, a small town near Avila, Spain. It was there that he learned this very important lesson about life: love is the most important thing of all. He learned this from the example of his parents—Gonzalo de Yepes and Catherine (aka Catalina) Alvarez—who were married in spite of the extreme displeasure of Gonzalo's family, and their threat to disown him if he were to marry beneath their social estate.

Gonzalo's family followed through on their threats after he married Catherine, and he and his young bride began their life together in abject poverty. Though he worked hard, the family remained very poor and food was scarce. Soon after John's birth, Gonzalo contracted a contagious disease as the result of an epidemic that swept through Spain during the sixteenth century, and this resulted in his untimely death. Barely a toddler, John was now fatherless; but not really so, for he sensed that another Father was waiting for him, and it was not long thereafter that he began his earnest quest for Him.

From his older brothers and his mother John learned many wonderful things about his earthly father, but the most important thing he learned was that in the face of true love everything else must be cast aside. No consideration is as important as that of love. This truth motivated John throughout his life, regardless of the circumstances he faced.

It's not surprising, therefore, that when John grew up, he fell in love with God, and most of his writings describe his pilgrimage to union with the love of God. It was not in any respect an easy journey for him, but he persevered and ultimately found the "pearl of great price," which Jesus describes in one of His parables: "Again, the kingdom of heaven is like unto a merchant man, seeking goodly pearls: who, when he had found one pearl of great price, went and sold all that he had, and bought it" (Matthew 13:45–46).

Saint John of the Cross truly gave all that he had in search of that great pearl—union with God through love. For several months he was even imprisoned for his faith and his desire to bring reformation to the Church. He experienced rejection, hatred, strife, illness, misunderstanding, and persecution, but he persevered in the face of all these negative influences, and they did not deter him from his goal. The devil set many snares for him, but he managed to overcome them all, as you will see in his penetrating descriptions of the spiritual battles every ardent soul must face.

The Song of Solomon proved to be a rich source of guidance and insight for him as he sought union with his Beloved, and he alludes to this book over and over again in both his prose and poetry. He saw himself (and each one of us, as well as all of us together) as the bride in search of her Beloved—the bride who sang: "Draw me, we will run after thee: the king hath brought me into his chambers: we will be glad and rejoice in thee, we will remember thy love more than wine: the upright love thee" (Song of Solomon 1:4). This devoted bride was ever diligent in her search for her Beloved, because: "A bundle of myrrh is my wellbeloved unto me; he shall lie all night betwixt my breasts. My beloved is unto me as a cluster of camphire in the vineyards of En-gedi. Behold, thou art fair, my love; behold, thou art fair; thou hast doves' eyes. Behold, thou art fair, my beloved, yea, pleasant: also our bed is green" (Song of Solomon 1:13–16).

This bride was seeking consummation in total union with her Beloved: "My beloved is mine, and I am his: he feedeth among the lilies ... By night on my bed I sought him whom my soul loveth: I sought him, but I found him not. I will rise now, and go about the city in the streets, and in the broad ways I will seek him whom my soul loveth: I sought him, but I found him not" (Song of Solomon 2:16–3:2). Eventually the bride found him whom her soul so long had sought—her Bridegroom and her Beloved, and it was the same for Saint John of the Cross, as he continued his search for union with God.

The trials and tribulations he went through became the substance of the spiritual purgation he underwent and the spiritual fodder for his poems and commentaries, which serve as a great example for every Christian who wants to know God more intimately and personally. Such a relationship, as Saint John points out, requires death to the self-life and overcoming all the Seven Deadly Sins—lust, greed, pride, envy, wrath, sloth, and gluttony.

In order to get to know God more intimately, one must surrender his or her life, possessions, desires, goals, and aspirations to Him. This is not an easy process, and for some of us, it can take a very long time, indeed; but for those who desire to do so, this book will serve as an extremely helpful guide.

Kieran Kavanaugh writes this about Saint John of the Cross:

"The Bible was the book he cherished most of all; he loved to withdraw to hidden parts of the monastery with his Bible. The Gospels, chiefly, helped him to enter into intimacy with the three persons of the Trinity. He so fully understood that in His Son the Father had spoken and revealed everything and that hidden in Christ were all the treasures of the wisdom and knowledge of God. There was no need for him, therefore, when he was in Lisbon, to accompany a group of friars on a visit to the famed stigmatic who lived in that city; he had his Bible, and he remained reading and reflecting upon it along the shore of the sea while his companions went off to satisfy their curiosity.

"Finally, his nearness to God filled him with confidence and freed him in a remarkable way from all worry and anxiety. Some of the monasteries where he was Prior were very poor, and this frequently caused his religious no little concern. But Fray John's confidence in God was so great during the times of want that he even hesitated to allow the procurator of the monastery to go out and beg for food. This complete trust in Providence, this habit of seeing the hand of God in all things, contributed to an air of peace and calm in the monastery. [This is very similar to the faith and confidence of a later Christian servant—George Mueller—who always trusted God for the needs of his orphans.] One feast day the brother cook let a pot of rice boil over and burn. Far from becoming angry, Fray John quietly consoled the brother, 'Don't worry, my son; we can have whatever else you've got. Our Lord does not mean us to have rice today.' This was his way, too, in persecution. He saw the hand of God there and exhorted others not to speak uncharitably or to grow disturbed about his persecutors, but to think 'only that God ordains all.' He taught that trust in God should be so great that even if the whole world were to collapse and come to an end one should not become disturbed. The endurance of all with peaceful equanimity, he wrote, not only reaps many blessings but helps a man in the midst of his adversity to make the proper judgment and apply the right remedy. This complete trust in God led him perfectly at peace in his final illness, and when someone reminded him of all he had suffered, he replied with these remarkable words: 'Padre, this is not the time to be thinking of that; it is by the merits of the blood of our Lord Jesus Christ that I hope to be saved.'"

The example of Saint John of the Cross continues to live in his works of prose and poetry from which one can glean a great deal about trust, faith, love, confidence, hope, and dedication.

We have taken the liberty to update the language of his poetry and commentaries in such a way that the modern reader will be able to relate to these more personally and with greater comprehension. The work of several translators has been helpful in this process, not the least of which is E. Allison Peers.

After examining several translations, it's interesting to note that different translators have gleaned different meanings from some of the writings of Saint John of the Cross. One of the reasons for this is that all languages—including Spanish and English—change over time. Meanings change. Emphases change. Sentence structure changes, and usage changes.

Some words broaden in meaning over time, while other words narrow in meaning. Certain idioms in one language are often difficult to translate into another language. In view of all these factors, we have spent considerable time examining various translations of Saint John's writings in an effort to come up with modern applications of his meanings in an easy-to-follow format.

In no case have we used any one translator's words exclusively or verbatim. Instead, we have combined the meanings of several translators. The result is a deeply spiritual work that will endure as a true Christian classic for many generations to come.

We have also provided a glossary in the back of the book, which provides definitions for certain terms that may be of a particularly theological nature or are considered archaic in our contemporary culture. So please refer to the glossary if any words are unfamiliar to you. We have also striven to make the language gender-inclusive.

To enhance the book's readability, we have shortened the paragraphs as often as possible and have added subheadings throughout the book. This will enable the reader to take time to meditate on the multitude of topics that Saint John of the Cross presents to us.

I am confident that you will be inspired and thrilled as you read the works that are contained within this book. They were written by a man who always put God first in his life. His writings will stir your heart with new spiritual understanding and a greater desire to know God in all His fullness.

I conclude this foreword with a fitting prayer that was written by Saint Paul. It is my prayer for you, because it asks God to bring about in your life the very things that Saint John of the Cross desired for his life and yours, as well:

> "For this cause I bow my knees unto the Father of our Lord Jesus Christ, of whom the whole family in heaven and earth is named, that he would grant you, according to the riches of his glory, to be strengthened with might by his Spirit in the inner man; that Christ may dwell in your hearts by faith; that ye, being rooted and grounded in love, may be able to comprehend with all saints what is the breadth, and length, and depth, and height; and to know the love of Christ, which passeth knowledge, that ye might be filled with all the fullness of God. Now unto him that is able to do exceeding abundantly above all that we ask or think, according to the power that worketh in us, unto him be glory in the church by Christ Jesus throughout all ages, world without end. Amen" (Ephesians 3:14–21).

Lloyd B. Hildebrand
Senior Editor
Bridge-Logos Publishers

References

The Collected Works of St. John of the Cross, translated by Kieran Kavanaugh, OCD, and Otto Rodriguez, OCD, published by OCD Publications, 1979, General Introduction.

"John of the Cross," from Wikipedia, the Free Encyclopedia. (http://en.wikipedia.or/wik/John_of_the_Cross)

"John of the Cross: The Person, His Times, His Writings by Michel Dodd, O.C.D. (http://www.icspublications.org/archives/others/cs6_4.html)

"John of the Cross" (http://www.chatoli-forum.com/Saints/saintj23.htm)

"Saint John of the Cross" (http://www.philosophyprofessor.com/philosophers/saint-john-of-the-cross.php)

"St. John of the Cross" (Catholic Encyclopedia—http://www.newadvent.org/cathen/08480.htm)

"St. John of the Cross" by Thomas Merton. (http://www.cin.org/saint/jcross-merton.html)

"Saint John of the Cross" (http://www.britannica.com/eb/article-9043815/Saint-John-of-the-Cross)

"Saint John of the Cross, Priest and Doctor of the Church (http://www.carmelites.ie/Saints/johnofthecross.htm)

The Complete Works of St. John of the Cross, Doctor of the Church, Translated from the Critical Edition of P. Silverio de Santa Teresa, C.D. and Edited by E. Allison Peers. (The Newman Bookshop, Westminster, Maryland, 1946).

The Fellowship of the Saints. Compiled by Thomas S. Kepler. Abingdon-Cokesbury Press, New York, Nashville, 1948.

Saint John of the Cross
1542–1591

BIOGRAPHY

SAINT JOHN OF THE CROSS

Whosoever will come after me, let him deny himself,
and take up his cross, and follow me.
For whosoever will save his life shall lose it;
but whosoever shall lose his life for my sake
and the gospel's, the same shall save it.
For what shall it profit a man, if he shall gain the
whole world, and lose his own soul?
(Mark 8:34-36)

THE EARLY YEARS

Saint John of the Cross was born in Fontiveros, Spain, near Avila, on June 24, 1542 (the Feast of the Nativity of Saint John the Baptist). His original name was Juan de Yepes y Alvarez; he was named in honor of Saint John the Baptist. He was the youngest child of Gonzalo de Yepes and Catherine (aka Catalina) Alvarez, who were poor silk weavers in the city of Toledo, Spain; they had to struggle and work very hard just to make ends meet.

Juan's father had come from a wealthy family, but he had been disinherited and rejected by them because he married a woman who was of a lower rank than that of his family. Soon after Juan's birth, Gonzalo died in the prime of his life, as a result of one of the pestilences that swept through Spain during the sixteenth century, leaving a destitute and grieving widow and three starving sons. His illness had lasted

1

for a couple of years and his medical care had been quite costly. With the help of her oldest son, Francisco, Catherine somehow managed to provide for the bare necessities of her family.

Catherine tried to obtain help from her husband's family, but to no avail. She first appealed to a brother-in-law who was an archdeacon in Torrijos, near Toledo. He made excuses and closed the door in the widow's face. Then she went to another one of her husband's brothers, who was a doctor in nearby Galvez. This man agreed to adopt Francisco, Catherine's oldest son. The adoption did not last long, however, because the doctor's wife soon began to abuse Francisco.

Before long, Catherine's middle son Luis died, probably of malnutrition. This convinced the grieving mother that she had to find better employment for herself and improved living conditions for her family, so she moved to Medina del Campo, a thriving market town. She continued to be a weaver there and taught the craft to her son, Francisco, who helped earn money for the family, as he worked with her.

The family continued to struggle with poverty, however, and moved from place to place in order to find better living conditions. This led young Francisco into petty thievery and vandalism for a while. He would wander the streets with his friends at night, playing the guitar and singing until the early morning hours. He would often fall asleep in church, not because he would go there to pray, but he had to "sleep off" his drunkenness.

Out of fear and guilt, Francisco sought the counsel of a priest, who was very helpful to him; and prayer, instead of drinking, revelry, stealing, and vandalism, became his way of life. Eventually he married Ana Izquierda, and Francisco settled down into a respectable and hard-working lifestyle—a life that was devoted to serving the needs of others.

All members of the family had become simple peasants who were engaged in a fight for survival. In spite of their poverty, Catherine's family was well-known for its charity toward others who were experiencing needs not unlike their own.

Francisco, for example, would go through the city streets and find hungry, homeless people and take them home with him so they could share the family's meager food and shelter with others. His devotion to Christ became obvious to all. The family made it their special mission, also, to rescue abandoned babies and take them into their own care or find others who could provide for them. In order to do this, they would beg for alms in the streets.

Francisco's religious convictions were vibrant and strong, and undoubtedly this must have made a lasting impression on his younger brother, Juan. Through all this struggle and turmoil young Juan surely learned many things about life's priorities. It is clear, for example, that he learned about the importance of love from his mother and brother (and from what he had learned about his father, as well).

Schooling

Eventually Juan was sent to a school for impoverished children at Medina del Campo. This was a type of boarding school for boys that provided basic reading and writing, the study of the catechism, and preparation for one of the trades. There he proved to be an outstanding pupil who was both attentive and diligent.

This school was established as a result of a growing government concern about wayward children. In 1548 the Parliament wrote, "For it is certain that by finding help for these lost children, robberies and serious and enormous crimes will be prevented. If these children are left to go free without a guide, such crimes will increase."

In many ways this school resembled an orphanage, for most of the students were poor, urban, illiterate, untrained, and undisciplined. Except for being poor, these depictions did not apply to Juan, however. While at the school Juan was chosen to be an acolyte at the Convent of the Augustinian Nuns. He began his duties in this role at 4:00 in the morning, and frequently had to serve as an altar boy in the afternoons as well.

A bit later, however, he was apprenticed to an artisan; this was a difficult assignment for Juan, because he was better at intellectual pursuits than he was at working with his hands. He tried his hand at carpentry, tailoring, sculpturing, and painting through apprenticeships with local craftsmen; though he tried hard in each of these apprenticeships, he was never successful at any. Francisco said that Juan's mother had "... tried to place her youngest son where he would learn a trade, and after trying carpentry, tailoring, carving, and painting, Juan did not settle into any of them; although he was fond of helping his mother with her work [weaving]."

This being the case, the governor of the hospital of Medina, Don Alonso, took Juan into his service; and for seven years the young man spent his time as a hospital orderly, helping to meet the needs of very poor people, many of whom suffered from the plague and various venereal diseases. He distinguished himself by his gentleness with the patients and his obvious love and concern for them.

Seeing his attitude and devotion, Don Alonso decided to help Juan with his education, so he enrolled him in a school that was run by the Jesuits, members of the Society of Jesus, which was a relatively new order within the Roman Catholic Church. It had been founded by Saint Ignatius Loyola in 1537. Juan proved himself to be outstanding in the area of verbal skills, and reading and writing seemed to come easy to him.

Juan was eighteen years old when he began attending the Jesuit school (from 1559 to 1563). The major focus of his studies there was upon the humanities. He diligently studied grammar, rhetoric, Greek, Latin, and religion. Many of his instructors were highly acclaimed in their fields. His grammar and rhetoric teacher, Padre Bonifacio, explained his relationship with his students as follows: "I lecture without any difficulty on Valerius Maximianus, Suetonius, Aliciatus; I explain some passages from Ammianus Marcelinus, Pliny, and Pomponius Mela; I translate some difficult passages from the Breviary including some of the hymns, also the Catechism, the letters of St. Jerome, and the proceedings of the Council of Trent. To my non-clerical pupils I lecture on Cicero, Virgil, and sometimes Seneca's tragedies, Horace and Martial unexpurgated, Caesar, Sallust, Livy, and Curtius, that they might have examples and models of everything: speeches, poetry, and history." Juan was well-trained in religion, language, and culture, as well.

After his studies in this school had been completed, Don Alonso offered to help Juan prepare for the priesthood. In this way, he thought that when Juan became ordained, he could serve as hospital chaplain, which would provide some money for him, his brother, and his mother. However, John felt a different call upon his life—he believed that God was leading him to enter a religious order.

GOD'S CALL

One thing thou lackest: go thy way, sell whatsoever thou hast, and give to the poor, and thou shalt have treasure in heaven: and come, take up the cross, and follow me.
(Mark 10:21)

There were at least two times in young Juan's life when he barely escaped death. These experiences gave him some anxiety about his future life. While praying, he was told that he was being called to serve God in an ancient order of the Catholic Church—the Carmelites. In 1563 Juan went secretly

to a recently founded Carmelite monastery in Santa Ana where he asked to receive the habit of Our Lady of Mount Carmel.

The spiritual focus of the Carmelite Order has always been on contemplative prayer, which held great attraction for Juan. The Carmelite Order derives its name from Mount Carmel, where a community of hermits lived and prayed some time after the ancient prophets of Israel lived there. The official name of the Carmelites is the Order of Our Lady of Mt. Carmel. Records indicate that the Carmelites had their origin sometime during the thirteenth century. (For more about the Carmelites, please refer to Chapter 4 of this book, which provides a good overview of the order and its history.)

Juan formally entered the Carmelite Order at Medina del Campos, Spain, on February 24, 1563, and in 1564, after making his profession, he continued his studies at the University of Salamanca and the Colegio de San Andres. He majored in philosophy. At this time he also began to teach.

One of the greatest influences in young John's life at that time was a particular professor at the university, Luis de Leon, who was one of the leading authorities in biblical studies during that era. From him Juan learned about biblical exegesis, and under this professor's tutelage, he also learned Hebrew and Aramaic.

Luis de Leon had translated the Old Testament book known as the Song of Solomon into Spanish. Surely John had read his teacher's translation of the Old Testament book, and the Song of Solomon (which is also known as the Song of Songs or Canticle of Canticles) greatly influenced his theology and writing in later years.

As a monk, Juan adopted the name of Juan de Santo Matia (John of Saint Matthias). After his profession of Holy Orders, Juan received permission from his superiors to follow the strictest rule of the Carmelite Order.

As a student, John of Saint Matthias was appointed to be Prefect of Studies, a position that was given to only the most extraordinary scholars. As such, he had to teach class daily, defend his theses publicly, and help the Regent Master find solutions to problems and objections that were raised. It became clear that John was a natural-born leader.

As a novice, John fervently threw himself wholeheartedly into the observance of the religious practices of his order. Even then he greatly appreciated solitude, and he was deeply devoted to prayer and to penance. Other monks admired John, but he was not considered to be popular by them. Some of them thought his zeal was too extreme. One thing was clear; John was one monk who would abide by the order's motto: "With zeal have I been zealous for the Lord God of Hosts."

In spite of all these experiences, successes, and the great zeal he had to find God, John was not completely happy. He had received permission to follow the strictest rule of his community, but this was not enough for him. He felt rather isolated from his peers, and in later life he wrote these words: "The virtuous soul that is alone and without a master is like a lone burning coal; it will grow colder rather than hotter. Those who fall alone remain alone in their fall, and they value their souls little since they entrust it to themselves alone. If you do not fear falling alone, do you presume that you will rise up alone? Consider how much more can be accomplished by two together than by one."

Following his preparation and his studies, John was ordained as a priest in 1567. While celebrating his first mass in his home monastery of Santa Ana, a brother student suggested that he might want to visit a certain nun who was in Medina arranging for the building of a new Carmelite monastery of nuns. This nun was none other than Teresa of Jesus (later known as Saint Teresa of Avila), who had been formerly known as Teresa de Ahuma da y Cepeda. Teresa had founded a reformed community of nuns in Avila in 1562.

Teresa of Jesus had begun to establish more houses of strictly enclosed nuns who were dedicated to following the more primitive rule of their order—the European Rule. They devoted themselves to contemplation and intercession for the Church. These sisters wore a simple habit, and they wore sandals on their feet that were symbolic of their devotion to the poor. They called themselves "Discalced Carmelites," a name that was derived from the Spanish word *descalzas*, which means "barefoot." Hence, they became known as "barefoot Carmelites" or Discalced Carmelites.

Around this time John received the assurance that he should preserve his baptismal innocence. It was at this point that he decided he would like to join the strict Carthusian Order because of its stress on solitary and silent contemplation; however, the earlier suggestion by a brother within his order led him in an entirely different direction.

SAINT TERESA'S INFLUENCE IN JOHN'S LIFE

I am crucified with Christ: nevertheless
I live; yet not I, but Christ liveth in me:
and the life which I now live in the flesh
I live by the faith of the Son of God,
who loved me, and gave himself for me.
(Galatians 2:20)

Before he was able to follow through on his idea to join the Carthusians, John met Teresa de Jesus; she persuaded the young priest to remain in the Carmelite Order, so he could assist her with the foundation of a monastery for friars who would be devoted to the strict and primitive rule of the Carmelites.

Here is what Teresa said about John: "And when I spoke with this young friar, he pleased me very much. I learned from him how he also wanted to go to the Carthusians. Telling him what I was attempting to do, I begged him to wait until the Lord would give us a monastery and pointed out the great good that would be accomplished if in his desire to improve he were to remain in his own order and that much greater service would be rendered to the Lord. He promised me he would remain as long as he wouldn't have to wait long." With this assurance from Teresa, John returned to Salamanca for one more year of studies.

In order to learn more about what she was proposing, John accompanied Teresa on a trip to Valladolin in the summer of 1568. By so doing he was able to gain practical experience in the manner of life that was practiced by the nuns who were cloistered there. It was Teresa's desire that John would "... have a clear understanding of everything, whether it concerned mortification or the style of both our community life and the recreation we have together. He was so good that I, at least, could have learned much more from him than he from me. Yet this was not what I did, but I taught him about the lifestyle of the sisters."

Throughout his twenties, John worked as Teresa's helper by cooperating with her in the founding of monasteries throughout Spain. He also took an active role in the government of those monasteries. His efforts were met with some resistance on the part of certain friars, however, especially those who did not desire to practice the stricter version of the order that Teresa and John advocated. Some of these men even tried to keep Teresa from entering their monasteries.

The Teresian Reform Movement

As we mentioned earlier, the reformed followers of Teresa and John became known as "Discalced" (barefoot or shoeless) Carmelites, which symbolized their identification with poverty, as opposed to those who were known simply as the "Calced" Carmelites. By use of the term "discalced," the reformed Carmelites indicated their commitment to voluntary poverty and living a life of austerity.

Teresa wrote about John in a letter to a friend:

> "... the Lord seems to be leading him by the hand, for, although we have had a few disagreements here over business matters, and I have been the cause of them, and have sometimes been vexed with him, we have never seen the least imperfection in him. He has courage."

These Discalced Carmelites lived very simple lives. John, for example, chose to live in a small hovel, which was an abandoned and dilapidated farmhouse. Even Teresa said the building was unfit for human habitation and that no one could bear to live in such a place. Nonetheless, John was joined by an ex-prior and a lay brother, Anthony de Heredia, who took up residence in the shack along with him.

John brought his family to live and work at the monastery. His mother and his sister-in-law helped with domestic duties, and his beloved brother, Francisco, helped with the maintenance of the property.

It was then that John began to call himself "John of the Cross," and he became the first master of novices there. Then he filled various posts in different places until Teresa called him to Avila to serve as Director and Confessor to the Convent of the Incarnation over which she was the Prioress. He remained in that role for five years.

In this capacity John taught his friars how to give themselves to a simple life of contemplation and reflection. They were very poor, but they enjoyed a great sense of community.

John of the Cross served in a variety of roles in the following years. He became the First Novice Master of the Reform. He established the novitiate at a new monastery in Pastrana. In 1571 he went to Alcala de Henares to found a house of studies for friars who were preparing to be ordained. In his work with students he always reminded them, "You are a religious and a student, but a religious first."

In October 1571, Teresa was sent back to the Monastery of the Incarnation in Avila. This was the institution that she had left to begin the Reform Movement. The superiors there wanted her to help rebuild the community, because it had fallen into economic and spiritual stagnation. Immediately, Teresa enlisted the help of John to work with her there.

John became a spiritual guide to the nuns who were there, and under his tutelage the nuns grew in the grace and knowledge of the Lord. John spent hours giving personal attention to the sisters, and he gave them the guidance they needed in following the Lord as dedicated Carmelites.

Though Teresa left there in 1573, John continued his work at the monastery until 1577. He lived with another friar in a small hermitage near the convent.

During this period great tensions continued to build between the Discalced Carmelites and the Calced Carmelites. John had become a symbol of the Discalced Carmelites and, as such, he became a leading target of the opposition's venomous attacks.

TORTURE AND IMPRISONMENT

For unto you it is given in the behalf of Christ, not only to believe on him, but also to suffer for his sake.
(Philippians 1:29)

The rift between the Calced and Discalced Carmelites widened, and this caused many problems for the members of both groups. On the night of December 3, 1577, John was ordered by his provincial to return to the house of his profession in Medina, but the young priest refused to obey this order.

Therefore, he was taken prisoner and transported to Toledo, where he suffered greatly through the diabolical punishment of isolation in a narrow, tiny cell that had previously served as a latrine; it was a veritable closet with hardly any light or air. It was a very cold and dank dungeon during cold spells, and a very hot and humid oven during hot spells.

This little room was barely big enough to contain his body, and he was tortured in various other ways as well. His captors kept him under a very harsh, strict, and brutal regimen, which included public whippings every week before the community. The purpose of all this was to cause John to change his views of the religious life, which he never did. He bore the scars of those beatings throughout the rest of his life.

What little food he was given consisted mainly of bread, sardines, and water. On three evenings each week he had to eat his meal while kneeling on the floor of the refectory in front of the friars. Then, when they had finished eating, John's shoulders were bared and each member of the community would strike him with a lash. Some would do so with sadistic strength and vigor.

He spent his time in prison by mentally composing poetry and committing it to memory. Though his cell was dark and gloomy, he was able to imagine pleasant scenes from nature—meadows, streams, mountains, flowers, beaches, and greenery. These reflections must have given him great peace and comfort, and they reappear in much of his poetry.

John compared his experience of imprisonment in Toledo to Jonah being in "the belly of the whale." While he was there, however, unlike Jonah he did not try to defend himself. He dealt with God alone, and God dealt with him. He waited patiently for a divine answer that would end the "dark night of the soul," which he was surely experiencing.

It was while John was in prison that he composed a large portion of his most famous poem, *Spiritual Canticle*, in which he reflects on the horrific conditions he had to endure. Many of his later works also allude to his experiences in prison.

In the midst of his sufferings, John was visited with heavenly consolations in a variety of forms. These divine encounters helped to sustain him during the most difficult circumstances of his life.

Realizing that he had little hope of release, John eventually decided to escape from prison by tying strips from a blanket together to make a rope that would enable him to climb down to safety. At the time of his daring escape he had been incarcerated for nine months.

John found his way to the Discalced nuns of Toledo, who hid him from the search party. Eventually he went to El Calvario in the southern part of Spain, where he was able to recuperate and regain a measure of strength.

In October 1578, the Discalced Fathers began another chapter at Almodovar. They elected John of the Cross as the Prior of the monastery of El Cavario. There was a strong, negative reaction to this from the new Nuncio, Felipe Sega, who violently declared that the resolutions were null and void, and he placed the Discalced friars under the jurisdiction of the Calced Carmelites. In the process he sent many of the fathers away to prison, but John went to El Calvario to assume his new position as Prior.

John also acted as Spiritual Director and Confessor for the nuns at Beas, but their Prioress, Madre Ana de Jesus, neither recognized John's holiness nor his talents. Therefore, she wrote a letter of complaint to Teresa, who responded with these words:

"I am really surprised, daughter, at your complaining so unreasonably, when you have Padre Fray John of the Cross with you, who is a divine, heavenly man. I can tell you, daughter, that since he went away I have found no one like him in all Castile, nor anyone who inspires people with so much fervor on the way to heaven. You would not believe how lonely his absence makes me feel. You should reflect that you have a great treasure in that holy man, and all those in the convent should see him and open their souls to him, when they will see what great good they get and will find themselves to have made great progress in spirituality and perfection, for our Lord has given him a special grace for this.

"I can assure you I should very much like to have Fray John of the Cross here, for he is indeed the father of my soul, and one of those whom it does me most good to have dealings with. I hope you and your daughters will talk to him with the utmost frankness, for I assure you that you can talk to him as you would to me, and you and they will find great satisfaction, for he is very spiritual and of great experience and learning. Those who were brought up on his teaching miss him greatly. Give thanks to God who has arranged that he should be near you. I am writing to tell him to look after you and I know that in his great kindness he will do so whenever the need arises."

Madre Ana soon realized that what Teresa had written was true. After his escape from prison, John continued with his work of reforming the Carmelites and founding and governing additional monasteries at Baeza, Granada, Cordova, Segovia, and elsewhere. However, he did not play a prominent role in the negotiations which led to the establishment of a separate government for Discalced Carmelites.

On March 3, 1581, John became Prior of the monastery at Granada. In addition to his administrative duties there, he worked manually to get the monastery and its grounds in better shape. While serving in Granada, he completed most of his poems and major treatises, although some of his works were never completed.

Throughout these years, he spent a great deal of time in prayer. Tempests between the Discalced and Calced Carmelites continued to affect him and others within the order. John was not hesitant to voice his opposition to what was taking place, and he did so twice to the Vicar General. This resulted in him not being elected to any office in 1590. In response to this he wrote these words to Madre Ana de Jesus (who was also under great opposition): "... If things did not turn out as you desired, you ought rather to be consoled and thank God profusely. Since His Majesty has so arranged matters, it is what most suits everyone ... And it is obvious that this is not evil or harmful, neither for me nor for anyone. It is in my favor since, being freed and relieved from the care of souls, I can, if I want and with God's help, enjoy peace, solitude, and the delightful fruit of forgetfulness of self and of all things. It is also good for others that I be separated from them, for thus they will be freed of the faults they would have committed on account of my misery ... Now, until God gives us this good in heaven, pass the time in the virtues of mortification and patience, desiring to resemble somewhat in suffering this great God of ours, humbled and crucified. This life is not good if it is not an imitation of His life. "

THE ILLNESS OF SAINT JOHN

But what things were gain to me, those I counted loss for Christ. Yea doubtless, and I count all things but loss for the excellency of the knowledge of Christ Jesus my Lord: for whom I have suffered the loss of all things, and do count them but dung, that I may win Christ, and be found in him.
(Philippians 3:7-9)

In mid-September 1591, John came down with a slight fever that was caused by an inflammation in one of his legs. He went to Ubeda in order to recuperate, but was not treated very well there, because the Prior of Ubeda, Fray Crisostomo, did not like him. The Prior was unfriendly toward John and gave him the worst cell in the monastery, all the while complaining about the expense his care was costing! Perhaps it was John's holiness that vexed him most.

16

Meanwhile, John's sickness worsened and his legs became ulcerated. Then the disease spread to his back, where a tumor that was larger than a man's fist began to grow.

While he was ill, one of John's opponents traveled from monastery to monastery in an effort to get monks to discredit him and take action against him. They were hoping for John's complete expulsion from the branch of the order that he had helped to found.

As John grew sicker and weaker, and the inflammation in his leg turned to gangrene, one of his constant prayers expressed his desire "to suffer and to be despised," and it seemed that it was being answered at Ubeda.

At long last, however, those who had been so ardently against John began to mellow and even some of his worst adversaries began to acknowledge his sanctity. John desired complete solitude by this time, because his physical health continued to deteriorate, and he must have sensed that he was dying.

On the evening of December 13, 1591, the end of John's life was very near, and he must have known this was so, for he called for the Prior and begged him for forgiveness for all the trouble and expense he had caused. The Prior responded by seeking John's forgiveness, and he left his cell in tears.

Next, John listened to some verses from the Canticle of Canticles (the Song of Solomon), and then prepared himself for his passage from this life to the next. When midnight came, the bells rang for matins, and John asked, "What are they for?"

The monks told him that the bells were announcing morning prayers, and he responded with these words, "Glory be to God, for I shall say them in heaven." Then he kissed his crucifix and said, "*Domine, commendo spiritum meum*—into your hands, O Lord, I commend my spirit." He was only forty-nine years old when he took his last breath.

He died on December 14, 1591, in Ubeda, Spain. When he died, many poor people went to see his body and to kiss his hands and his feet. Some even tore pieces from his habit as tokens of remembrance. For a while his burial site had to be concealed from the public, many of whom revered him deeply. The church kept his relics at Segovia.

His deeply spiritual writings were published posthumously in 1618. These works were written primarily for the religious and for any who deeply love God and desire to follow Him. One editor of his work, E. Allison Peers, writes this tribute to Saint John of the Cross:

> The Cross is the staff whereby one may reach him [Saint John], and whereby the road is greatly lightened and made easy. Wherefore our Lord said through St. Matthew: My yoke is easy and my burden is light, which burden is the Cross. For if a man resolve to submit himself to carrying his cross, that is to say if he resolve to desire in truth to meet trials and to bear them in all things for God's sake, he will find in them great relief and sweetness wherewith he may travel on this road, detached from all things and desiring nothing.

The "dark night of the soul" that Saint John of the Cross had to go through in order to die to himself and achieve union with Christ was the cross itself. This was the focal point of his life, and it is clear that he was willing to take up his cross and follow his Lord and Master, the One he loved with all his heart. Saint John shows us that total detachment is possible when one surrenders his or her life to Jesus Christ, denies himself or herself, and surrenders all to the Lord.

Saint John writes about his spiritual experiences in the midst of suffering with these stirring words:

"These times of aridity cause the soul to journey in all purity in the love of God, since it is no longer influenced by its actions, by the pleasure and sweetness of the actions themselves ... but only by a desire to please God. It becomes neither presumptuous nor self-satisfied, as perchance it was wont to become in the time of its prosperity, but fearful and timid with regard to itself, finding in itself no satisfaction whatsoever; and herein consists that holy fear which preserves and increases the virtues. ... Save for the pleasure indeed, which at certain times God infuses into it, it is a wonder if it find pleasure and consolation of sense, through its own diligence, in any spiritual exercise or action. ...There grows within souls that experience this arid night (of the senses) care for God and yearnings to serve him, for in proportion as the breasts of sensuality, wherewith it sustained and nourished the desires that it pursued, are drying up, there remains nothing in that aridity and detachment save the yearning to serve God, which is a thing very pleasing to God." (From *Dark Night of the Soul*.)

This paragraph reveals the heart of St. John of the Cross to us. It shows us what he wanted most from life—a detachment from self that would enable him to serve God, know God, and please God, a detachment so complete that it would find its complete fulfillment in union with God.

The famous Trappist monk and author, Thomas Merton, considered St. John of the Cross to be the most accessible of all the saints. He writes, "If I say that St. John of the Cross seems to me to be the most accessible of the saints, that is only another way of saying that he is my favorite saint together with three others who also seem to me most approachable:

St. Benedict, St. Bernard, and St. Francis of Assisi. After all, the people you make friends with are the ones who welcome you into their company. But besides this, it also seems to me that St. John of the Cross is absolutely and in himself a most accessible saint. This, to those of you who find him forbidding, will seem an outrageous paradox. Nevertheless it is true, if you consider that few saints, if any, have ever opened up to other men such remote depths in their own soul. St. John of the Cross admits you, in the Living Flame, to his soul's 'deepest center,' to the 'deep caverns' in which the lamps of fire, the attributes of God, flash mysteriously in metaphysical shadows; who else has done as much? St. John reveals himself to us not in allegory, as does St. Teresa, but in symbol. And symbol is a far more potent and effective medium than allegory. It is truer because it is more direct and more intimate. It does not need to be sorted out and applied by the reason. The symbols that spring from the depths of the heart of St. John of the Cross awaken kindred symbols in the depths of the heart that loves him. Their effect, of course, is supported and intensified by grace which, we may believe, the saint himself has begged for the souls of those who have been called to love him in God. Here is a union and a friendship than which nothing could be more intimate, except the friendship of the soul with God himself. Earth knows no such intimacies ... And thus St. John of the Cross not only makes himself accessible to us, but does much more: he makes us accessible to ourselves by opening our hearts to God within their own depths."

THE LITERARY WORKS OF
SAINT JOHN OF THE CROSS

*That I may know him, and the power of
his resurrection, and the fellowship of his
sufferings, being made conformable unto his death.
(Philippians 3:10)*

Saint John of the Cross is considered to be one of the foremost poets within the Spanish language. His two most famous poems—*The Spiritual Canticle* and *Dark Night of the Soul* (both of which are included in their entirety in this book)—are widely considered to be among the best poems ever written in Spanish. They employ various elements of literature in vivid and compelling ways.

The Spiritual Canticle is an allegory in which the soul (represented as a bride) searches for her bridegroom (Christ), experiences anxiety over having lost Him, and finds great joy when they are reunited. In this poem we see the profound influence of the Song of Solomon in Saint John's poetry.

Dark Night of the Soul utilizes the journey motif to show how the soul leaves its bodily home in order to find union with God. This happens during the darkness of night, and the soul encounters numerous challenges, conflicts, hardships, and difficulties that must be faced and overcome in order to become detached from the world and gain union with God.

A third work, *Ascent of Mount Carmel*, shows the steps one must go through in order to achieve perfect union with God and the mystical experiences one will encounter along the way. Regarding the chronology of these poems, it's important to note that *Ascent of Mount Carmel* should precede *Dark Night of the Soul.*

A fourth work, *Love's Living Flame*, which is included in its entirety in this book, involves the soul's longing for total

21

intimacy with God. This happens through purgation of both sense and spirit, and it results in the joys of abundant and eternal life with God. As a result, the soul becomes a living flame within the fire of God's love.

Cardinal Wiseman says about Saint John of the Cross that he "... invents nothing, borrows nothing from others, but gives us clearly the results of his own experience in himself and others. He presents you with a portrait, not with a fancy picture. He represents the ideal of one who has passed, as he had done, through the career of the spiritual life, through its struggles and its victories."[15]

The following is a list of many of the works of St. John of the Cross:

• "The Ascent of Mount Carmel." Originally, this work was to have been completed in four books, but it stops in the middle of the third book.

• *Dark Night of the Soul.* This work, along with the preceding one, was written soon after John escaped from prison. Both works complement each other by forming a fairly thorough treatise regarding mystical theology.

• "Spiritual Canticle." The title is derived from the Canticle of Canticles (the Song of Solomon or the Song of Songs). It was begun during his imprisonment, but was not completed until some years later, when Venerable Anne of Jesus urged St. John to finish the work.

• "Love's Living Flame." (aka "O Living Flame of Love.") This poem was written around 1584 in response to Dona Ana de Penalosa's request.

• He wrote a manual of spiritual instructions and precautions.

• Approximately twenty of his letters, which were chiefly written to his penitents, are extant. His other letters, including his correspondence with St. Teresa, were unfortunately destroyed. John got rid of many of these letters himself when he was going through various persecutions.

• Twenty-six of his poems have been published.
• Numerous other minor works.

THE CORE OF SAINT JOHN'S TEACHING

Verily, verily, I say unto you,
Except a corn of wheat fall into the ground and die,
it abideth alone: but if it die, it bringeth forth much fruit.
He that loveth his life shall lose it; and he that hateth his
life in this world shall keep it unto life eternal.
(John 12:24–25)

Saint John of the Cross clearly believed that the soul must empty itself of the self-life in order to be filled with God, and that it has to be purified of all dross that is accumulated from living in this world. He writes, "Substantial union with God is that by which the soul exists." He explains the use of the word "night" as follows:

"Night is the image for the dark journey of detachment as the soul actively purges herself of desires for that which is specific, concrete and particular and as God purges her of desires and dependencies."

Saint John clearly teaches that suffering is integral to finding union with God and that love is both "the mode and content of knowing" Him. He wrote three works regarding mystical theology. These works have greatly influenced other spiritual writers, including T.S. Eliot, Edith Stein (who was canonized as Saint Teresa Benedicta of the Cross), Thomas Merton, and Therese de Lisieux.

23

Saint John of the Cross believed that substantial union with God is what enables the soul of a person to exist. He taught that it was possible for the soul to become like God through what he called "the union of likeness," a transforming or mystical union. He believed that the soul had to travel through darkness in order to find union with God; he called this journey the *via negativa*. He viewed suffering as God's purging that enables us to become detached from the things of this world as well as from the self.

In *Dark Night of the Soul*, Saint John of the Cross reveals the process through which the soul becomes detached. This happens as the soul experiences the Crucifixion of Christ.

It is clear that St. John loved the Word of God and knew many Scriptures by heart, the fruit of his meditational and contemplational style of Bible reading, and he was greatly influenced by Saint Thomas Aquinas's *Summa Theologiae* as well.

Saint John of the Cross was beatified by Pope Clement X on January 25, 1675. He was canonized by Pope Benedict XIII on December 27, 1726. He was proclaimed to be a Doctor of the Church by Pope Pius XI on August 24, 1926.

The Character of Saint John of the Cross

All of the experiences that Saint John of the Cross went through, from the earliest stages of his life to his death, might have turned the average person into a bitter cynic. In John's case they turned him into a true saint, one who found immense possibilities everywhere and one who was able to extract positive things from negative experiences. In this sense he was very much like Joseph, who told his brothers, "But as for you, ye thought evil against me; but God meant it unto good, to bring to pass, as it is this day, to save much people alive" (Genesis 50:20).

From his writings and the writings of those who knew him we can glean a great deal about the character and spiritual life of Saint John of the Cross.

Though he was very small in stature (approximately five feet tall), *Saint John of the Cross was a true giant of the faith.* He had compassion for the poor, which must have stemmed from the poverty that he and his family were so familiar with. He understood the Bible, which says, "Blessed is he that considereth the poor: the **LORD** will deliver him in time of trouble. The **LORD** will preserve him, and keep him alive; and he shall be blessed upon the earth: and thou wilt not deliver him unto the will of his enemies" (Psalm 41:1–2).

Saint John of the Cross had a deep concern for those who were sick and dying. His experiences in the hospital in Medina helped him to develop a deep sense of empathy for those who suffered and were in pain. The Bible says, "And when he had called unto him his twelve disciples, he gave them power against unclean spirits, to cast them out, and to heal all manner of sickness and all manner of disease" (Matthew 10:1).

Saint John of the Cross understood the emotional and psychological disturbances in others as well, and he spent a great portion of his life trying to relieve sadness and depression in others. Though he was a very serious person by nature, he enjoyed making others laugh. He knew the Bible, which says: "A merry heart doeth good like a medicine; but a broken spirit drieth the bones" (Proverbs 17:21).

Saint John of the Cross was a true gentleman, even when he had to administer correction or discipline to others. In fact, he often asked, "Who has ever seen men persuaded to love God by harshness?" Within the fruit of the Holy Spirit we find gentleness: "But the fruit of the Spirit is love, joy, peace, longsuffering, gentleness, goodness, faith, meekness, temperance: against such there is no law" (Galatians 5:22–23).

Saint John of the Cross possessed great confidence that stemmed from faith and trust. This confidence came directly from God and was an outgrowth of Saint John's constant pursuit of closeness with his Father in Heaven. The Bible says, "And this is the confidence that we have in him, that, if we ask any thing according to his will, he heareth us: and if we know that he hear us, whatsoever we ask, we know that we have the petitions that we desired of him" (1 John 5:14–15).

Saint John of the Cross was a man of faith and trust, which were built upon the solid foundation of his knowledge of the Scriptures. He believed the following verses with all his heart: "Trust in the **LORD** with all thine heart; and lean not unto thine own understanding. In all thy ways acknowledge him, and he shall direct thy paths" (Proverbs 3:5–6).

Saint John of the Cross possessed a great love for nature. He loved to spend time in nature and to take his fellow monks with him so that they would gain a new perspective on life. The Bible says, "The heavens declare the glory of God; and the firmament sheweth his handywork" (Psalm 19:1).

Saint John of the Cross loved other people—his family, his co-laborers, his friends, and his enemies. The Bible says, "Beloved, let us love one another: for love is of God; and every one that loveth is born of God, and knoweth God" (1 John 4:7).

Saint John of the Cross loved God. Indeed, loving God was the theme of his life. He knew these words of the Scriptures: "There is no fear in love; but perfect love casteth out fear: because fear hath torment. He that feareth is not made perfect in love. We love him, because he first loved us" (1 John 4:18–19).

Saint John of the Cross loved the Word of God. His Bible was his constant companion. God's Word was life to him. The Bible says, "Thy word is a lamp unto my feet, and a light unto my path" (Psalm 119:105).

We conclude this all-too-brief biographical sketch of Saint John of the Cross with a tribute that was written by Thomas Merton, a twentieth-century Trappist monk:

"John of the Cross is the patron of those who have a vocation that is thought, by others, to be spectacular, but which, in reality, is lowly, difficult, and obscure. He is the patron and the protector and master of those whom God has led into the uninteresting wilderness of contemplative prayer. His domain is precisely defined. He is the patron of contemplatives in the strict sense, and of their spiritual directors, not of contemplatives in the juridical sense. He is the patron of those who pray in a certain way in which God wants them to pray, whether they happen to be in the cloister, the desert, or the city. Therefore his influence is not limited to one order or to one kind of order. His teaching is not merely a matter of 'Carmelite spirituality,' as some seem to think. In fact, I would venture to say that he is the father of all those whose prayer is an undefined isolation outside the boundary of 'spirituality.' He deals chiefly with those who, in one way or another, have been brought face to face with God in a way that methods cannot account for and books do not explain. He is in Christ the model and the maker of contemplatives wherever they may be found."

The Convent of Santa Teresa, Avila

TIME LINE OF THE AUTHOR'S LIFE

Saint John of the Cross: His name means "God is gracious; gift of God."

June 24, 1542: Born as Juan de Yepes at Fontiveros, Spain.

1549: The death of Juan's father.

1552–1556: Juan attended school at the Colegio de los Ninos de la Doctrina in Medina.

February 24, 1563: At the age of twenty-one Juan became a Carmelite brother in the Monastery of Santa Ana, Medina del Campo, as Juan de San Matias (Juan of Saint Matthew).

1564: Juan continued his studies at the University of Salamanca and the Colegio de San Andres. (He took a three-year course in the arts.)

1567: At the age of twenty-five, Juan was ordained as a Roman Catholic priest.

Summer 1568: John of the Cross accompanied Teresa on a trip to Valladolin. He spent part of the summer at Duruelo, Median, and Avila.

November 28, 1568: John inaugurated the Reform of Discalced Carmelites among his fellow-friars. He was joined in taking these vows by Antonio de Heredia (Antonio de Jesus), Prior of the Calced Carmelites at Medina; and Jose de Cristo, another Carmelite from Medina.

1570: The Duruelo Monastery was transferred to Mancera. In October, John founded the second monastery of the Reform at Pastrana.

1571: John founded a House of Studies for friars who were preparing for ordination at Alcala de Henares. This is the third monastery of reform that he founded, and he directed the Carmelite nuns here as well. In October 1571, Teresa of Avila became the Prioress of the Convent of the Incarnation in Avila. She remained in this office until 1573. John began to work with Teresa again in the rebuilding of the community at the Monastery of the Incarnation in Avila.

1572: John became Confessor to the Convent of the Incarnation.

1572–1577: This was a period of open hostility between the Calced and Discalced Carmelites.

1573: Teresa left Avila, but John remained there until 1577.

December 3, 1577: John was arrested, then imprisoned in the Calced Carmelite Monastery in Toledo, Spain.

1577–1578: John of the Cross composes several stanzas of the "Spiritual Canticle" and one of his poems, "Dark Night of the Soul."

August 15, 1578: John of the Cross escaped from prison as the result of a vision he had received. He went to the convent of the Carmelite nuns in Toledo.

October 1578: John was elected as the Prior of the Monastery of El Cavario. He attended a Chapter General of the Discalced at Almodovar. Was sent to Monte Calvario as Vicar. During this same month a papal decree submitted the Discalced Carmelites to the Calced.

1578–1579: John began his commentary on *The Ascent of Mount Carmel* and the *Spiritual Canticle*.

June 14, 1579: John founded a house of the Reform at Baeza.

1579–1581: John resided at Baeza as Rector of the Carmelite House. He wrote more of his prose works and the final stanzas of *Spiritual Canticle* during this time, as well.

June 22, 1580: The Discalced Reform was recognized by a bull from Pope Gregory XIII.

March 3, 1581: John became Prior of the Monastery at Granada.

October 15, 1582: The death of Teresa of Avila.

1582–1588 – John of the Cross was the Prior at Granada. During this period he wrote the last five stanzas of "The Spiritual Canticle," finished the *Ascent of Mount Carmel*, and composed his remaining prose works.

May 1, 1583: The Provincial Chapter of Almodovar took place.

1585: John of the Cross wrote "Love's Living Flame" in fifteen days at the request of Dona Ana de Penalosa. In this same year the Chapter of Lisbon, which divided the Discalced Province into four vicariates, took place. Saint John of the Cross became Vicar-Provincial of Andalusia. He continued founding monasteries: San Jose de Malaga; Cordoba; Manholes de Jaen; Caravaca, and Bujalance.

June 27, 1587: The new Constitution of the Reform was published.

1588: John of the Cross was made Prior of the Monastery of Segovia, which became the Central House of the Reform.

June 1590: John of the Cross was re-elected first Consiliario at the Chapter of Madrid.

June 1591: John of the Cross was deprived of his offices and was elected Provincial of Mexico, but this appointment was subsequently revoked.

July 1591: John of the Cross went to La Penuela.

September 1591: John of the Cross was attacked by a fever. He left La Penuela for Ubeda.

December 14, 1591: John of the Cross died at Ubeda, Andalusia, Spain.

January 25, 1675: John of the Cross was beatified by Pope Clement X.

December 27, 1726: Saint John of the Cross was canonized by Pope Benedict XIII

August 24, 1926: Saint John of the Cross was proclaimed Doctor of the Church Universal by Pope Pius XI.

References

The Complete Works of St. John of the Cross, Doctor of the Church. Translated from the Critical Edition of P. Silverio de Santa Teresa, C.D. and Edited by E. Allison Peers. (The Newman Bookshop, Westminster, Maryland, 1946.)

The Collected Works of St. John of the Cross, translated by Kieran Kavanaugh, OCD and Otilio Rodriguez, OCD. (Published by ICS Publications, Institute of Carmelite Studies, Washington, DC, 1979).

The Fellowship of the Saints, compiled by Thomas S. Kepler, Abingdon-Cokesbury Press, New York, Nashville, 1948.

"St. John of the Cross" by Thomas Merton. (http://www.cin.org/saints/jcross-merton.html)

"John of the Cross" (http://en.wikipedia.org/wiki/John_of_the_Cross)

"Saint John of the Cross" (http://www.philosophyprofessor.com/philosophers/saint-joh-of-the-cross.php)

"John of the Cross" (http://www.catholic-forum.com/Saints/saintj23.htm)

"Saint John of the Cross, Priest and Doctor of the Church" (http://www.carmelites.ie/Saints/johnofthecross.htm)_

"Saint John of the Cross" (http://www.britannica.com/eb/article-9043815/SAint-John-of-the-Cross)

"St. John of the Cross" (http://www.newadvent.org/cathen/08480a.htm)

"John of the Cross: the Person, His Times, His Writings" by Michael Dodd, OCD. (http://www.icspublications.org/archives/others/cs6_4.html)

THE CARMELITES

And he [Elijah] *came thither unto a cave, and lodged there;*
and, behold, the word of the LORD *came to him,*
and he said unto him, What doest thou here, Elijah?
And he said, I have been very jealous for the LORD
God of hosts: for the children of Israel have forsaken
thy covenant, thrown down thine altars, and slain thy
prophets with the sword; and I, even I only, am left;
and they seek my life, to take it away.
(1 Kings 19:9–10. This took place just prior to
Elijah's ascent of Mount Carmel.)

Mission Statement

The Carmelite Order of the Roman Catholic Church had
its origins during the Middle Ages, as did many other Catholic
religious orders. The origins of the order are somewhat hazy,
but it would appear that it began on Mount Carmel (near
present-day Haifa, Israel), where some hermits who lived in
caves spent their lives studying the Scriptures, doing manual
labor, and praying. We will deal more with the order's history
a bit later.

The Carmelites' contemporary mission statement is:

"We embrace an eighth century contemplative,
prophetic tradition of Gospel living, patterned on
the Carmelite Rule and inspired by Elijah and Mary.

As contemplatives, we seek to live consciously in the presence of God and to affirm and challenge one another by living a prayerful life in common. As prophets, we walk with people, announcing God's presence, denouncing oppression, and promoting the well-being of the human family, as we serve in pastoral, educational, spiritual, and other creative ministries in the United States, Canada, Mexico and Peru."

Organization of the Order

Like many medieval Roman Catholic orders, the Carmelites consist of three different divisions or orders:

- The First Order—the active/contemplative friars.
- The Second Order—the cloistered (or enclosed) nuns.
- The Third Order—laypeople who live in the world. (Unlike members of the first two orders, members of the third order can be married. They participate in the order by way of the liturgy, prayers, ministries and, most especially, contemplative prayer.)
- There are offshoots of the order as well, such as the active Carmelite sisters.

Mount Carmel

The Bible tells of many amazing things that happened on Mount Carmel and the region surrounding it. The Carmelites trace their origins back to Mount Carmel, which is located near Haifa, Israel. This is where Elijah heard the still small voice of the Lord. (See 1 Kings 19:12).

Elijah had challenged the people to choose either God (Yahweh) or Baal, and he was able to demonstrate the power of God when his sacrifice was consumed by fire: "And it came to pass at the time of the offering of the evening sacrifice, that Elijah the prophet came near, and said, LORD God of

Abraham, Isaac, and of Israel, let it be known this day that thou art God in Israel, and that I am thy servant, and that I have done all these things at thy word. Hear me, O LORD, hear me, that this people may know that thou art the LORD God, and that thou hast turned their heart back again. Then the fire of the LORD fell, and consumed the burnt sacrifice, and the wood, and the stones, and the dust, and licked up the water that was in the trench. And when all the people saw it, they fell on their faces: and they said, The LORD, he is the God; the LORD, he is the God.

And Elijah said unto them, Take the prophets of Baal; let not one of them escape ... And Elijah said unto Ahab, Get thee up, eat and drink; for there is a sound of abundance of rain" (1 Kings 18:36–41).

At this time Elijah was a very solitary figure; indeed, he felt that he was the only Israelite who had not bowed his knee to Baal. He told God that he was jealous for Him, and he prayed for a miracle, which God promptly provided. Elijah and the Israelites saw a remarkable display of God's living presence and His awesome power that day.

When Jezebel heard about the things that Elijah had done, she threatened his life. Elijah then went into the wilderness. Weary, depressed, and probably fearful, he sat down beneath a juniper tree, and he said that he wanted to die. He prayed, "Now, O LORD, take away my life; for I am not better than my fathers" (1 Kings 19:4). Then he fell asleep.

An angel of the Lord came to him, touched him, and told him to get up and eat and drink. This is when the prophet ascended Mount Carmel and heard the gentle voice of God speaking to him. God told him to return to the valley, now that he was refreshed, and to continue prophesying to the people.

The Carmelites have derived much from the example of Elijah, a servant of the Most High God who loved to experience His presence, delighted in solitude, spent much time in prayer, and felt compelled to minister to others. This is the mission of the Carmelites, as well—to descend the mountain of God and minister to the people in the valley.

In the same way that Elijah experienced the living God and was able to practice His presence, the Carmelites endeavor to encounter and recognize God in everyone they meet and serve. They seek to practice God's presence every day of their lives, no matter where they are.

They recognize the need to spend time on the mountaintop in solitude and prayer, but they also know the importance of going into the valleys where people need their help.

The experience of Elijah is very much like that of the soul described by Saint John of the Cross in *Dark Night of the Soul*—a solitary figure who has to endure great suffering in the wilderness before finding God on top of the mountain.

Elijah is one of the two great figures who have inspired Carmelites throughout the centuries. The other figure is Mary, the mother of Jesus. Both of these figures are human models of what Carmelites aspire to become—contemplative, active, prayerful, prophetic, reflective, and apostolic—Christians who seek God above all else.

Both Elijah and Mary knew what it feels like to be alone, to experience fear, to face difficult questions, and to know the hurts that others can cause; but both persevered in God and both became triumphant, as they placed their lives in God's hands. Both are models of contemplation as well. As such, these two children of God serve as great examples for Carmelites to follow.

The Early History of the Order

During the time of the Crusades in the Middle Ages, religious hermits settled in various places throughout Palestine. Some of these men adopted a solitary lifestyle on Mount Carmel, near a spring called Elijah's Fountain. They lived in small cells that were similar to those in a beehive, and there they gathered "the divine honey of spiritual consolation." It is believed that these monks were the successors to the "sons of the prophets" in ancient Israel.

The "sons of the prophets" resembled more modern monastic communities in many ways. They led a communal life and they dedicated themselves to God's service. They submitted to their superiors in obedience and devotion. It is believed that Elijah and Elisha may have been their earliest leaders.

Both of these prophets were directly connected to Mount Carmel, and Elisha actually lived there for an extended period of time; however, the downfall of the Kingdom of Israel caused the "sons of the prophets" to leave that region.

Later, in the third or fourth century, Mount Carmel became a place where Christian pilgrims would go to spend time alone with God. Saint John the Baptist spent most of his life in the desert surrounding this region, and some believe that he and his disciples revived the "sons of the prophets" on Mount Carmel. Jesus said that His cousin, John the Baptist, was endowed with the spirit and virtue of Elijah.

Though there is no one single founder of the Carmelite Order, some people give credit to a twelfth-century monk who is known as Saint Bertold, but it was the hermits we referred to above who are considered to be the actual founders of the order. These hermits surrendered everything to God and consecrated themselves to the One who shed His blood for them. It was their desire to serve Jesus Christ, and they did so by living in voluntary poverty and by forming a religious community. They spent their time in prayer, contemplation, and manual labor.

The Greek monk John Phocas visited the Holy Land in 1185, and he said that he met a monk on Mount Carmel. He reported that this monk, with the help of about ten other hermits, had built a monastery there. The monk had stated that he had experienced an apparition of the prophet Elijah, which prompted him to begin a community.

These hermits lived in shared solitude and began to care for one another. In approximately 1206, these brothers asked the Patriarch of Jerusalem, Albert, to draw up a way of life in the form of a rule for them. Albert presented a Rule of Life to them in 1214 (part of which had been adapted from the Rule of Augustine), in which he directed the hermits to celebrate the Eucharist each day and to gather in weekly meetings for encouragement and correction. There were sixteen articles in this rule, which include the following:

> These men were directed to elect a prior to whom they were to promise obedience. They were to live apart from each other, in cells. They were to spend time in prayer and manual labor each day. They were to have no personal property and they were to be vegetarians, unless sickness would require them to eat meat. They were expected to fast from the middle of September until Easter. Many Carmelites follow these same rules today.

This rule received the approval of Pope Honorius III in 1226. Soon afterward the hermits were forced to flee the mountain; they eventually migrated to various parts of Europe, including Sicily, England, France, Spain, and Italy.

Saint Teresa of Avila and Saint John of the Cross

Teresa of Avila became sick soon after she took religious vows in 1535. Consequently she spent most of her time in prayer and contemplation. It became her deep desire to live a more perfect life and to see the primitive rule of the Carmelite Order restored. Therefore, she founded a convent in her native town. In fifteen years she founded sixteen additional convents of nuns, and this was done in the face of fierce opposition from those who did not agree with her.

John of the Cross, who had just completed his studies, began to work with Teresa, along with another friar, Anton de Heredia. These men embarked on a challenging journey that included many hardships and difficulties. This is when the name "Discalced Carmelites" began to be used to represent monks and nuns who were devoted to the strictest rule of the order, the same rule that the hermits had followed on Mount Carmel. Teresa of Avila and John of the Cross were great leaders in this Teresian Reform Movement.

The Calced Carmelites appealed to Rome, and a great dislike of the Reform Movement began to grow. Many Discalced Carmelites, including John of the Cross, were imprisoned and tortured. This persecution lasted nearly a year, until King Philip II intervened and put a stop to it.

The Discalced Carmelites were inspired with asceticism and a sense of devotion that was quite uncommon in those days. In 1593 they had their own general, and by 1600 they were so numerous that it became necessary to divide them into two congregations—the congregations of Spain and Italy.

The Carmelite Way

In his book, *The Carmelite Way*, John Welch, O.Carm., writes:

> "Carmel learned to tell the story of the human heart as a love story. Thinking they were searching for something missing in their lives, Carmelites discovered they were being pursued by a loving Presence whose desire for them gave them increased life, greater freedom, and a trustworthy relationship for their guidance."

The Carmelite Way, therefore, is a way of life that involves prayer, contemplation, service, and community. The practice of the presence of God is extremely important to them. While being contemplatives, they reach out to the world with the love of God.

Welch writes, "A prayerful life, lived in community, and generously serving others has remained a constant Carmelite ideal."

Modern Carmelites

Things began to decline for the order during the seventeenth and eighteenth centuries. By the closing decades of the nineteenth century there were only 200 Carmelite men in the world. A resurgence of interest in the order began around the turn of the twentieth century, and this resulted in new leadership and less political interference. The theological preparation of the Carmelites was strengthened when Saint Albert's College was founded in Rome.

By 2001 the membership had increased to approximately 2,100 men in twenty-five provinces, 700 enclosed nuns in seventy monasteries, and thirteen affiliated congregations and institutes.

The Discalced Carmelite Order is still represented atop the Carmel Mountain Range at the Muhraka Monastery, which is located near Haifa, on the eastern side of Mount Carmel. It stands on the foundations of earlier monasteries. The name of the monastery—*Muhraka*—means "place of burning," and this is a reference to the encounter between Elijah and the priests of Baal. (See 1 Kings 18:20–40.)

Major Carmelite figures of the twentieth century include: Saint Therese of Lisieux, one of the few female doctors of the Church. She is famous for her teaching on the "Little Way" of confidence in God; Titus Brandsma, a Dutch scholar and writer who was killed in the Dachau Concentration Camp because of his stance against Nazism; Saint Theresa Benedicta of the Cross (nee Edith Stein), a Jewish convert to Catholicism who was imprisoned by the Nazis and died at Auschwitz. In addition, Saint Raphael Kalinowski (1835–1907) became the first Carmelite friar to be sainted since Saint John of the Cross was.

It's interesting to note that Brother Lawrence, who wrote *The Practice of the Presence of God*, was a Carmelite friar of the seventeenth century. A quote from his classic is an appropriate conclusion to this chapter, because it speaks of the devotion and contemplative lifestyle of the Carmelites:

> "You must know that the tender and loving light of God's countenance kindles imperceptibly within the soul that ardently embraces it, a fire of love to God that is so great and so divine that it is necessary for the person who is so affected to moderate the outward expression of their feelings. Great would be our surprise, if we but knew what communion the soul holds at these times with God. He seems to so delight in this communion, that to the soul who would willingly abide forever with Him, He bestows favors past numbering." (From *The Practice of the Presence of God* by Brother Lawrence.)

References

"Order of Carmelites, Tradition, Introduction. (http://www.carmelites.net/tradition/index.html)

The Carmelite Way by John Welch, O. Carm.

The Practice of the Presence of God by Brother Lawrence, Revised and Rewritten by Harold J. Chadwick, Published by Bridge-Logos Publishers, Orlando, Florida, 1999.

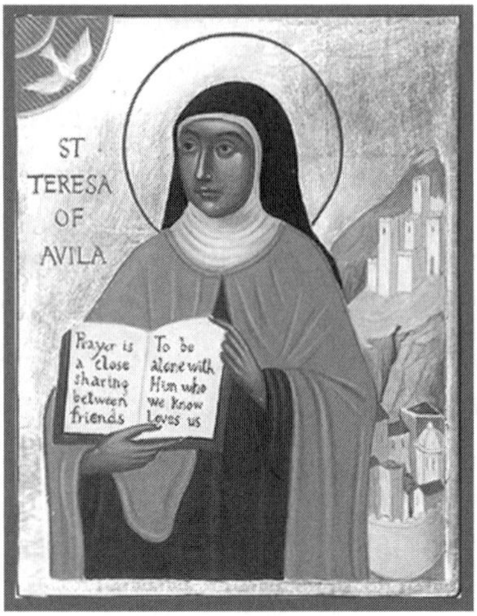

Text on book reads:
"Prayer is close sharing between friends …
To be alone with Him who we know loves us."

Text on scroll reads:
"My beloved is the mountains,
strong islands and resounding rivers."

SAINT TERESA OF AVILA—

CO-LABORER WITH JOHN OF THE CROSS

Finally, brethren, farewell. Be perfect,
be of good comfort, be of one mind,
live in peace; and the God of love
and peace shall be with you.
(2 Corinthians 13:11)

Saint Teresa's Early Life

We are including a brief biography of Saint Teresa of Avila here because she worked so closely with Saint John of the Cross in their attempt to bring reformation to the Carmelite Order and the Roman Catholic Church. Their kindred spirit was evident in both their work and their writings.

Teresa was born in Avila, Spain, on March 28, 1515. She was the third child of saintly Don Alonso Sanchez de Cepeda and Dona Beatriz Davila y Ahumada, who died when Teresa was only fourteen.

There were ten children in the family, and it is said that Teresa was the "most beloved of them all." She was considered to be a beautiful young lady. She possessed a buoyant and extroverted personality, was a good writer, and her work with needlework and domestic chores was outstanding.

She was devoted to the Lord from an early age. In fact, when she was only seven years of age, she and her brother Rodrigo left home with the intention of going into Moorish territory where they had hoped to be beheaded for Christ! Fortunately, their uncle prevented them from following through with this plan.

When Teresa's mother died, the young girl grew very depressed and began to spend much time in prayer. In 1531 her father, upon seeing her needs, sent her away to be with the Augustinian nuns at Santa Maria de Gracia.

Due to illness, however, she left the convent after being there for only eighteen months. For several years thereafter she remained with her father in Avila; she sometimes lived with her uncle as well. Her uncle introduced her to the letters of Saint Jerome, and, as a result of reading these, Teresa grew determined to adopt the religious life.

God's Call

Her father would not consent to her becoming a nun, however, so, unbeknownst to him, she left home and entered the Carmelite Convent of the Incarnation at Avila. For a while, she endured what seemed like death to her, because of the rift that had taken place within her family due to her choice to enter the religious life. Before long, however, her father accepted her choice and gave her his blessing.

After her profession in the following year, Teresa grew seriously ill. She went through a battery of medical tests and treatments, but these seemed to make matters worse. In fact, her health remained permanently impaired from then on.

Her father took her to Becedas, where a woman healer who was famous throughout the area lived, but Teresa's health did not improve. In July 1539, her father brought her back to Avila. Then in August of that year she lapsed into a coma, and many thought she was dying or that she might

46

even be dead already. Eventually, she experienced a bit of a cure, which she attributed to a miracle.

In her sickness, Teresa began to practice mental or contemplative prayer. She discontinued this for a while until she came under the influence of the Dominicans and the Jesuits. It was during this period of her life that God began to visit her with "intellectual visions and locutions."

During this period she was held back spiritually in some respects by her deep desire to be appreciated by others. This was finally put to rest when she experienced a radical conversion in the presence of "the sorely wounded Christ." Thus, at the age of thirty-nine Teresa began to enjoy a sense of God's presence wherever she went.

This was the beginning of Teresa's experience as a mystic. The spiritual manifestations she saw and heard were greatly impressed on her mind, and she said that these gave her great strength during times of trial. News of her visions spread far and wide, and some thought that they originated from the devil, not from God. Try as she might to resist them, the supernatural experiences continued and grew even stronger and more frequent. In August 1560, Peter of Alcantara gave this spiritual direction to Teresa: "Keep on as you are doing, daughter; we all suffer such trials."

Teresa writes about these experiences in her autobiography, *Life Written by Herself*, which was originally published in 1565. From this, one of her most famous works has been derived; it is called *Interior Castle* and is still in print today.

A Great Reformer

Teresa's desire for closer union with God through Christ and her hope for reformation in the Church began deeply within herself. She made a vow to follow a more perfect course, and she resolved to keep the rule of her order as faithfully as she possibly could. She joined with a group of

Discalced Carmelites under the direction of Peter of Alcantara; together, they planned for the foundation of a monastery. When these plans became known in the community, a great outcry arose among the townspeople and the secular and church leadership. Eventually, however, approval for the monastery was granted.

Toward the end of 1562, Teresa of Jesus was finally authorized by the Provincial to return to the new convent. Teresa reports that this ushered in the most peaceful five years of her life. During this time she wrote *The Way of Perfection* and her *Meditations on the Canticle*.

She began the work of establishing several foundations, convents, and monasteries throughout Spain in the years between 1567 and 1571.

In 1569 she passed through Duruelo, where John of the Cross and Anthony of Jesus had established the first convent of Discalced Brethren in November 1568. The following year Teresa established the second convent for Discalced Brethren in Pastrana.

Throughout these years both she and John of the Cross faced great opposition. John was a great help to Teresa during these times. He served as a confessor for the nuns and helped to bring about a great spiritual renewal among them.

Crisis within the Order

The General Chapter at Piacenza in 1575 ordered the Discalced Brethren to withdraw from Andalusia, and Teresa was ordered to retire to a convent. There was great bitterness within the Calced Carmelites toward the Discalced Carmelites of which Teresa and John were the leaders.

While the battle between the two factions raged, Teresa was in the convent continuing with her writing. She wrote a part of her greatest book, *The Interior Life*, while she was there, along with *The Foundations*. It was during this time that John of the Cross was imprisoned in Toledo.

After the crisis subsided somewhat, partly due to the intervention of the king, Teresa returned to visiting her convents and establishing new ones. The weakness and illness that had haunted her throughout her life was growing worse. Even though she was broken in health, she continued to work until the early autumn of 1582. In Alba de Torres she took to her bed and passed away on October 4, 1582.

Her Teachings and Her Writings

Teresa's four main works are: her autobiography, *The Relations, The Way of Perfection*, and *The Interior Castle*, which is also known as *The Interior Life*. Though these were written during various stages of her life, much of her theology and philosophy can be distilled from them.

She wrote extensively on the topic of prayer. She depicts different stages in the life of prayer by using a series of metaphors and analogies that are related to obtaining water in order to irrigate a garden. The first water is drawn from a well by someone carrying a bucket—a reference to the hard work and spiritual dryness that may accompany one who is just starting in the life of prayer. The second phase (the "second water") is where one begins to enter into contemplation and meditation—"the prayer of quiet," which she regarded as a gift from God through which the individual experiences the passive aspects of prayer. The third stage brings the seeker into what Teresa calls the "sleep of the faculties." The metaphor she employs for the fourth water is rain—a state of union in prayer.

In her works she stresses piety, integrity, asceticism, mysticism, prayer, intimacy with God, and love. She sees the soul ascending toward God in four stages:

- The "heart's devotion"—devout contemplation and concentration. The withdrawal of the soul from without and the devout observance of the Passion of Christ, followed by a penitent attitude.

49

- The "devotion of peace"— the human will is lost in God's will by way of a supernatural gift of God. The prevailing state is one of quietude.
- The "devotion of union"—a supernatural and ecstatic state. Human reason is absorbed into God. This stage is characterized by a blissful peace and a conscious rapture in the love of God.
- The "devotion of ecstasy or rapture"—a passive state in which the consciousness of being in one's body disappears. A negation of all the faculties occurs, as one finds complete union with God. The body is literally lifted into space, completely above the things of this world.

Tributes to Saint Teresa of Avila

She is venerated in both the Roman Catholic Church and the Lutheran Church, and is greatly admired by Christians of many denominations. On April 24, 1614, she was beatified by Pope Paul V. She became a patroness of Spain in 1617. Her canonization took place on March 12, 1622, by Pope Gregory XV. Her feast day is October 15. The Roman Catholic Church reveres her as the "seraphic virgin." In 1970, the Holy See designated her as a Doctor of the Church; she was the first woman to receive such an honor.

References

http://en.wikipedia.org/wiki/Teresa_of_Avila

http://www.karmel.at/eng/teresa.htm

http://www.newadvent.org/cathen/14515b.htm

Love's Living Flame

A Poem by Saint John of the Cross

O love's living flame—O fire of living love
With piercing heat Thou dost tenderly
wound my soul
Deep within my soul's deepest center!
Now You do not oppress me or evade me,
Now consummate if it be Your will:
And rend the veil of this sweet encounter!

O sweet burning wound,
O delightful and more-than-pleasant wound!
O soft and gentle hand! O touch most delicate
That reveals eternal life to me
And cancels every debt I owe!
Slaying all, you change death into life!

O lamps of fire that shine
With such an intense light and transparence,
The deep caverns of feeling wherein the senses live,
Which were once obscure and without sight,
Now with bright glories, give forth
Both heat and light to the Beloved's caresses.

How tame and loving, with benign intent,
You awaken in my heart sweet memories of You,
Where You abide in secret;
And in Your fragrant breathing,
Full of goodness and grace,
How delicately You swell my heart with love and
teach me to love.

THE SONG OF SOLOMON
KEY VERSES AND INSIGHTS

My beloved is mine, and I am his:
he feedeth among the lilies.
Song of Solomon 2:16

As a preface to *Dark Night of the Soul*, it is good for us to look briefly at the Song of Solomon (also known as the Song of Songs or the Canticle of Canticles), for it plays such a prominent role in all the writings of Saint John of the Cross.

The Song of Solomon is a love song/poem that is set in the blossoming of springtime. Though Solomon wrote more than 1000 songs, he must have considered this one to be his opus, for he calls it the Song of Songs. It is a celebration of marriage that is interpreted by many (including Saint John of the Cross) to represent the intimate, loving relationship between the Bride of Christ (the individual believer and the Church) and the Lord himself, who is the Bridegroom.

This is a magnificent poetic composition that is filled with vivid imagery, including abundant metaphors, similes, and extended analogies. It is a song that extols the joys and blessings of married life.

Both Jews and Christians see deep meaning in this book of the Bible. Jews read this poem at Passover as an allegory to the time when God said that He espoused Israel to himself as His bride.

Christians view this book as an allegory of the relationship between Christ and His Church, the beloved Bride of Christ. The following New Testament verses describe this blessed relationship:

- "And Jesus said unto them, Can the children of the bridechamber mourn, as long as the bridegroom is with them? but the days will come, when the bridegroom shall be taken from them, and then shall they fast" (Matthew 9:15).
- "Then shall the kingdom of heaven be likened unto ten virgins, which took their lamps, and went forth to meet the bridegroom" (Matthew 25:1).
- "He that hath the bride is the bridegroom: but the friend of the bridegroom, which standeth and heareth him, rejoiceth greatly because of the bridegroom's voice: this my joy therefore is fulfilled" (John 3:29).
- "For I am jealous over you with godly jealousy: for I have espoused you to one husband, that I may present you as a chaste virgin to Christ" (2 Corinthians 11:2).
- "For the husband is head of the wife, even as Christ is the head of the church: and he is the saviour of the body" (Ephesians 5:23).
- "Let us be glad and rejoice, and give honour to him: for the marriage of the Lamb is come, and his wife hath made herself ready" (Revelation 19:7).
- "And I John saw the holy city, new Jerusalem, coming down from God out of heaven, prepared as a bride adorned for her husband" (Revelation 21:2).
- "And the Spirit and the bride say, Come. And let him that heareth say, Come. And let him that is athirst come. And whosoever will, let him take the water of life freely" (Revelation 22:17).

CHAPTER ONE OF THE SONG— "YOUR LOVE IS BETTER THAN WINE"

The first chapter of the Song of Solomon expresses the bride's love for her Beloved, the Lord Jesus Christ. Let's listen to some of what she has to say about the budding relationship between her and her Beloved:

- "Let him kiss me with the kisses of his mouth: for thy love is better than wine" (Song of Solomon 1:2).
- "Because of the savour of thy good ointments thy name is an ointment poured forth, therefore do the virgins love thee" (Song of Solomon 1:3).
- "Draw me, we will run after thee: the king hath brought me into his chambers: we will be glad and rejoice in thee, we will remember thy love more than wine: the upright love thee" (Song of Solomon 1:4).
- "Tell me, O thou whom my soul loveth, where thou feedest, where thou makest thy flock to rest at noon: for why should I be as one that turneth aside by the flocks of thy companions" (Song of Solomon 1:7).
- "I have compared thee, O my love, to a company of horses in Pharaoh's chariots" (Song of Solomon 1:9).
- "Thy cheeks are comely with rows of jewels, thy neck with chains of gold" (Song of Solomon 1:10).
- "A bundle of myrrh is my wellbeloved unto me; he shall lie all night betwixt my breasts" (Song of Solomon 1:13).
- "My beloved is unto me as a cluster of camphire in the vineyards of En-gedi" (Song of Solomon 1:14).
- "Behold, thou art fair, my love; behold, thou art fair; thou hast doves' eyes" (Song of Solomon 1:15).
- "Behold, thou are fair, my beloved, yea, pleasant: also our bed is green" (Song of Solomon 1:16).

The above verses reveal the love that is felt for the soon-to-be bride for her Beloved, the King. She takes great delight in intimacy with Him and greatly appreciates His love for her. He fills her life with beautiful and pleasant fragrances and, as He draws her, she runs after Him. She is now searching for Him with all her heart, remembering how wonderful and pleasant He is and how good it is to be with Him.

CHAPTER TWO OF THE SONG— "HIS BANNER OVER ME IS LOVE"

This chapter continues with the delight the Bride experiences when she finds herself experiencing intimacy with her Beloved. Clearly she is delighted by the King's love for her, so she continues her search for union with Him—the inviolable union of holy matrimony.

- "As the apple tree among the trees of the wood, so is my beloved among the sons. I sat down under his shadow with great delight, and his fruit was sweet to my taste" (Song of Solomon 2:3).
- "He brought me to the banqueting house, and his banner over me was love" (Song of Solomon 2:4).
- "Stay me with flagons, comfort me with apples: for I am sick of [from] love" (Song of Solomon 2:5).
- "His left hand is under my head, and his right hand doth embrace me" (Song of Solomon 2:6).
- "I charge you, O ye daughters of Jerusalem, by the roes, and by the hinds of the field, that ye stir not up, nor awake my love, till he please" (Song of Solomon 3:5).
- "The voice of my beloved! behold, he cometh leaping upon the mountains, skipping upon the hills" (Song of Solomon 2:8).
- "My beloved is like a roe or a young hart: behold, he standeth behind our wall, he looketh forth at the

windows, shewing himself through the lattice" (Song of Solomon 2:9).

- "My beloved spake, and said unto me, Rise up, my love, my fair one, and come away" (Song of Solomon 2:10).
- "O my dove, that art in the clefts of the rock, in the secret places of the stairs, let me see thy countenance, let me hear thy voice; for sweet is thy voice, and thy countenance is comely" (Song of Solomon 2:14).
- "My beloved is mine, and I am his: he feedeth among the lilies" (Song of Solomon 2:16).
- "Until the day break, and the shadows flee away, turn, my beloved, and be thou like a roe or a young hart upon the mountains of Bether" (Song of Solomon 2:17).

In the above verses the bride-to-be is expressing her memories of being with her beloved, and she is looking for the time when she will be with Him forever. She compares Him to a dove, a roe, and a young hart—all images of peace and beauty. She describes His countenance as being handsome and strong. He is a vigorous and active man in whom she takes great delight, and she is very protective of Him.

CHAPTER THREE OF THE SONG— THE LOVER DISAPPEARS AND IS FOUND AGAIN

Seeking complete union with her Beloved, the bride-to-be searches everywhere until she finds Him. She begins this search at night. The joy she experiences in finding her Beloved is filled with excitement, happiness, and rejoicing.

- "By night on my bed I sought him whom my soul loveth: I sought him, but I found him not" (Song of Solomon 3:1).

- "I will rise now, and go about the city in the streets, and in the broad ways I will seek him whom my soul loveth: I sought him, but I found him not" (Song of Solomon 3:2).
- "The watchmen that go about the city found me: to whom I said, Saw ye him whom my soul loveth?" (Song of Solomon 3:3).
- "It was but a little that I passed from them, but I found him whom my soul loveth: I held him, and would not let him go, until I had brought him into my mother's house, and into the chamber of her that conceived me" (Song of Solomon 3:4).
- "I charge you, O ye daughters of Jerusalem, by the roes, and by the hinds of the field, that ye stir not up, nor awake my love, till he please" (Song of Solomon 3:5).
- "Who is this that cometh out of the wilderness like pillars of smoke, perfumed with myrrh and frankincense, with all powders of the merchant?" (Song of Solomon 3:6).
- "Go forth, O ye daughters of Zion, and behold king Solomon with the crown wherewith his mother crowned him in the day of his espousals, and in the day of the gladness of his heart" (Song of Solomon 3:11).

What did the bride-to-be do when she finally found her Lover, after searching for him all through the night? She held him and did not want to let him go. Clearly, she adores her Beloved, for whom she prepared a place of rest within her mother's house and cautioned all others not to disturb Him. Her description of Him in this passage is one of delightful fragrances and white pillars of smoke, which ascend to the heavens.

The bridal procession is about to begin, and the daughters of Zion—the palace ladies—will be the bridesmaids. The King will wear the crown His mother placed upon His head when

He was espoused to be married—a day of great rejoicing and gladness of heart for Him.

CHAPTER 4 OF THE SONG—
THE KING ADORES HIS BRIDE

The Beloved One is now turning His attention to His bride whom He obviously adores and loves very deeply. His descriptions of her in this chapter form some of the most stirring love imagery that has ever been written in poetry.

- "Behold, thou art fair, my love; behold, thou art fair; thou hast doves' eyes within thy locks: thy hair is as a flock of goats, that appear from mount Gilead" (Song of Solomon 4:1).
- "Thy teeth are like a flock of sheep that are even shorn, which came up from the washing; whereof every one bear twins, and none is barren among them. (Song of Solomon 4:2).
- "Thy lips are like a thread of scarlet, and thy speech is comely: thy temples are like a piece of a pomegranate within thy locks" (Song of Solomon 4:3).
- "Thy neck is like the tower of David builded for an armoury, whereon there hang a thousand bucklers, all shields of mighty men" (Song of Solomon 4:4).
- "Thy two breasts are like two young roes that are twins, which feed among the lilies" (Song of Solomon 4:5).
- "Thou art all fair, my love; there is no spot in thee" (Song of Solomon 4:7).
- "Thou hast ravished my heart, my sister, my spouse; thou hast ravished my heart with one of thine eyes, with one chain of thy neck" (Song of Solomon 4:9).

- "How fair is thy love, my sister, my spouse! how much better is thy love than wine! and the smell of thine ointments than all spices!" (Song of Solomon 4:10).
- "Thy lips, O my spouse, drop as the honeycomb: honey and milk are under thy tongue; and the smell of thy garments is like the smell of Lebanon" (Song of Solomon 4:11).
- A garden enclosed is my sister, my spouse; a spring shut up, a fountain sealed" (Song of Solomon 4:12).

Through the use of various similes and metaphors the King sings praises to His beloved bride. He says that she has ravished His heart and that she has the eyes of doves. Her teeth are like a flock of sheep and her lips are like a thread of scarlet. He admires her hair, her mouth, her neck, and her breasts, and He proclaims that He finds no spot or blemish on her body anywhere. (This is similar to what Saint Paul wrote about the relationship between Christ and the Church: "Therefore as the church is subject unto Christ, so let the wives be to their own husbands in every thing. Husbands, love your wives, even as Christ also loved the church, and gave himself for it; that he might sanctify and cleanse it with the washing of water by the word, that he might present it to himself a glorious church, not having spot, or wrinkle, or any such thing; but that it should be holy and without blemish" —Ephesians 5:24–27.) The Beloved finds no spot, wrinkle, or blemish in His greatly adored bride.

At the end of Chapter 4 the bride invites her Beloved into her garden, where there are many pleasant fruits, fragrances, fountains, wells, and winds. (See Song of Solomon 4:12–16.)

CHAPTER 5 OF THE SONG— A DREAM, A DISCOVERY, AND A RENEWED DEVOTION

In this chapter the bride dreams that her Lover has disappeared once more, and, though she searches for Him, she cannot find Him for the longest time. She anticipates a wonderful time of reunion when she does find him—a time of sweet union with her Beloved.

- "I sleep, but my heart waketh: it is the voice of my beloved that knocketh, saying, Open to me, my sister, my love, my dove, my undefiled: for my head is filled with dew, and my locks with the drops of the night" (Song of Solomon 5:2).
- "My beloved put in his hand by the hole of the door, and my bowels were moved for him" (Song of Solomon 5:4)
- "I rose up to open to my beloved; and my hands dropped with myrrh, and my fingers with sweet smelling myrrh, upon the handles of the lock" (Song of Solomon 5:5).
- "I opened to my beloved; but my beloved had withdrawn himself, and was gone: my soul failed when he spake: I sought him, but I could not find him; I called him, but he gave me no answer" (Song of Solomon 5:6).
- "I charge you, O daughters of Jerusalem, if ye find my beloved, that ye tell him, that I am sick of [from] love" (Song of Solomon 5:8).
- "My beloved is white and ruddy, the chiefest among ten thousand" (Song of Solomon 5:10).
- "His head is as the most fine gold, his locks are bushy, and black as a raven" (Song of Solomon 5:11).
- "His eyes are as the eyes of doves by the rivers of waters, washed with milk, and fitly set" (Song of Solomon 5:12).

- "His cheeks are as a bed of spices, as sweet flowers: his lips like lilies, dropping sweet smelling myrrh" (Song of Solomon 5:13).
- Hs hands are as gold rings set with the beryl: his belly is as bright ivory overlaid with sapphires" (Song of Solomon 5:14).
- His legs are as pillars of marble, set upon sockets of fine gold: his countenance is as Lebanon, excellent as the cedars" (Song of Solomon 5:15).
- "His mouth is most sweet: yea, he is altogether lovely. This is my beloved, and this is my friend, O daughters of Jerusalem" (Song of Solomon 5:16).

In her attempt to find her Beloved, the bride offers a vivid description of His appearance: she says He is white and ruddy, and she compares His head to gold, and says that His hair is as black as a raven. He had said that she had doves' eyes, and she declares that His eyes are like the eyes of doves as well. She employs olfactory and visual imagery to describe His cheeks—a bed of spices and flowers. His lips are like lilies and His hands are like gold rings set with a beryl stone. By saying that His legs are like pillars of marble, she is praising His strength and stability. Her handsome Bridegroom is "altogether lovely."

CHAPTER 6 OF THE SONG—
MY BELOVED IS MINE AND I AM HIS

Still searching for her Beloved, the bride continues to wonder where He has gone, and He begins to wonder what she might be doing. She continues her description of her Lover. Others join her in her wondering and in her search.

- Whither is thy beloved gone, O thou fairest among women? whither is thy beloved turned aside? that we may seek him with thee" (Song of Solomon 6:1)
- My beloved is gone down into his garden, to the beds of spices, to feed in the gardens, and to gather lilies" (Song of Solomon 6:2).
- "I am my beloved's, and my beloved is mine: he feedeth among the lilies" (Song of Solomon 6:3).
- "Thou art beautiful, O my love, as Tirzah, comely as Jerusalem, terrible as an army with banners" (Song of Solomon 6:4).
- "Who is she that looketh forth as the morning, fair as the moon, clear as the sun, and terrible as an army with banners?" (Song of Solomon 6:10).

The key verse in this chapter is verse 3: "I am my beloved's and my beloved is mine" (Song of Solomon 6:3). This verse implies total unity in love and possession. We are possessed by Christ; we are His, and He is ours.

CHAPTER 7 OF THE SONG— MUTUAL DEVOTION TO EACH OTHER

The awaited reunion has come, and the couple now lavishes in a renewed sense of unity, joy, and devotion. They luxuriate in each other's company and can see only good in each other.

- "How beautiful are thy feet with shoes, O prince's daughter! the joints of thy thighs are like jewels, the work of the hands of a cunning workman" (Song of Solomon 7:1).

- "Thy navel is like a round goblet, which wanteth not liquor: thy belly is like an heap of wheat set about with lilies" (Song of Solomon 7:2).
- "Thy two breasts are like two young roes that are twins" (Song of Solomon 7:3).
- "Thy neck is as a tower of ivory; thine eyes like the fishpools in Heshbon, by the gate of Bath-rabbim: thy nose is as the tower of Lebanon which looketh toward Damascus" (Song of Solomon 7:4).
- "And the roof of thy mouth like the best wine for my beloved, that goeth down sweetly, causing the lips of those that are asleep to speak" (Song of Solomon 7:9).
- "I am my beloved's, and his desire is toward me" (Song of Solomon 7:10).
- "Come, my beloved, let us go forth into the field; let us lodge in the villages" (Song of Solomon 7:11).
- "Let us get up early to the vineyards; let us see if the vine flourish, whether the tender grape appear, and the pomegranates bud forth: there will I give thee my loves" (Song of Solomon 7:12).

The bride and the Bridegroom are preparing to consummate their relationship in total unity that both have been seeking. It is clear that they are falling deeper and deeper in love and that their love must find fruition in total devotion to each other forever.

CHAPTER 8 OF THE SONG— UNQUENCHABLE LOVE AND INDISSOLUBLE UNION

"Each for the other" is now the theme of their lives—the theme of their life together. They vow that nothing shall quench their love from this point on.

- "His left hand should be under my head, and his right hand should embrace me" (Song of Solomon 8:3).
- "Set me as a seal upon thine heart, as a seal upon thine arm: for love is strong as death" (Song of Solomon 8:6a).
- "Many waters cannot quench love, neither can the floods drown it: if a man would give all the substance of his house for love, it would utterly be contemned" (Song of Solomon 8:7).
- "Make haste, my beloved, and be thou like to a roe or to a young hart upon the mountains of spices" (Song of Solomon 8:14).

John of the Cross employed the vivid imagery of the Song of Solomon to describe what the soul must go through in order to find unity with its Beloved, who is the Lord Jesus Christ. He became aware of the power of this book of the Bible when he was studying under Fray Luis de Leon, who taught biblical studies at the university in Salamanca, Spain. Leon was an expert in biblical studies, and he wrote an important and controversial translation of the Song of Songs into Spanish. (This was controversial, for translation of the Scriptures into vernacular Spanish was not permitted in Spain at that time.) John was greatly influenced by this translation, as his writings show.

As you read *Dark Night of the Soul*, you will see how the soul is very much like the bride in the Song of Solomon. Like her, the soul is on a quest, a somewhat frenetic search for its Beloved, and is willing to do anything to find Him. As the bride began her search in the dark, the soul must go through the "dark night of the soul" in order to achieve its goal—total union with the Savior.

In the process, the soul must go through many trials and tribulations, which include loss, deprivation, dryness, darkness, despair, detachment, and death to self and all things that had once given it pleasure. Likewise, the soul experiences emptiness, fear, uncertainty, and confusion along the way.

However, as Saint John of the Cross points out, through perseverance, faith, love, and devotion, the soul will eventually find its Beloved, as long as it is not distracted and does not turn back. The results will be complete transformation, union with God, and unspeakable joy.

References

"The Song of Solomon"—The *King James Version* of the Holy Bible.

THE SEVEN DEADLY SINS AND
THE SEVEN HOLY VIRTUES

Wherefore seeing we also are compassed about
with so great a cloud of witnesses, let us lay aside
every weight, and the sin which doth so easily beset
us, and let us run with patience the race
that is set before us.
(Hebrews 12:1)

The Tendency to Sin

Christian theology teaches that all human beings are born in sin as a result of the total depravity of mankind that was caused by the Fall of Adam and Eve in the Garden of Eden. Saint John of the Cross opens *Dark Night of the Soul* with a discussion of the Seven Deadly Sins (from a spiritual point of view), which the soul must overcome in order to enter into spiritual renewal and learn to walk in the Seven Cardinal Virtues through union with love—the love of God.

The Seven Deadly Sins are also known as the Seven Capital Vices or Seven Cardinal Sins. This depiction was provided by the Roman Catholic Church during the Middle Ages. At that time the church fathers classified sins by way of two divisions: *venial sins*, which are not deadly and are considered to be somewhat minor; these could be forgiven through the sacraments of the church. The *deadly sins*, however, are those which destroy the life of grace within the believer and carry with them the threat of eternal damnation unless they are absolved through confession and perfect contrition.

Let's begin by listing the Seven Deadly Sins, and then we will discuss each of them in terms of their effects upon the soul:

• *Luxuria*—This sin deals with luxury, extravagance, and in more recent times is most often associated with sexual lust.

• *Gula*—This sin deals with a lack of self-discipline, particularly with regard to eating and drinking. It stems from being immoderate, a lack of self-control, and the appetites of the flesh.

• *Avarita*—This sin is also known as avarice or greed. It involves a desire to have more and more and is often associated with extreme materialism.

• *Acedia*—Also known as sloth, this sin stems from laziness and indolence. It is named for an animal that is particularly known for its lack of energy and its slowness.

• *Ira*—This sin deals with extreme anger or wrath. It is the root word for "irate."

• *Invidia*—This sin is envy—a form of jealousy that relates to wanting what others possess and enjoy.

• *Superbia*—This sin is the sin of the kind of pride that the Greeks called *hubris*, a love of self that is so strong that it literally blinds those who live in it, because they think that they are superior to all others.

1. Luxuria—Lust

The following specific sins fall under this category: fornication, perversion, adultery, pedophilia, incest, use of pornography, bestiality, rape, sodomy, and any other sins of a lustful and sexual nature. This might also include obsessive or compulsive thoughts or desires of a sexual nature, including any kind of sexual addiction.

Often, those who are victimized by lust can be characterized as having what Dante called an "excessive love of others." This excessive preoccupation puts God no higher in their lives than second place. Sometimes victims of lust are confused about the difference between sex and love, and this causes major problems in their lives. Very frequently their chief goal in life is sexual release.

One of the major problems with this sin is that others may tend to be viewed as objects for sexual fulfillment—a means to an end—rather than as uniquely created individuals who are loved by God.

The following Bible verses deal with this particular sin:

"Ye have heard that it was said by them of old time, Thou shalt not commit adultery: But I say unto you, That whosoever looketh on a woman to lust after her hath committed adultery with her already in his heart" (Matthew 5:27–28).

"Wherefore God also gave them up to uncleanness through the lusts of their own hearts, to dishonour their own bodies between themselves" (Romans 1:24).

"But every man is tempted, when he is drawn away of his own lust, and enticed. Then when lust hath conceived, it bringeth forth sin: and sin, when it is finished, bringeth forth death" (James 1:14–15).

2. Gula—Gluttony

This sin may have both physical and spiritual forms. It relates to waste, overindulgence, and intemperance with regard to eating and drinking. Substance abuse, alcoholism, and binge drinking would fall under this category; as would eating disorders, such as anorexia nervosa and bulimia. It is marked by unreasonable or unnecessary consumption of food and drink.

The following Bible verses speak to this sin:

"When thou sittest to eat with a ruler, consider diligently what is before thee: and put a knife to thy throat, if thou be a man given to appetite. Be not desirous of his dainties: for they are deceitful meat" (Proverbs 23:1–3).

"Wine is a mocker, strong drink is raging: and whosoever is deceived thereby is not wise" (Proverbs 20:1).

"This I say then, Walk in the Spirit, and ye shall not fulfil the lust of the flesh" (Galatians 5:16).

3. Avarita—Greed and Avarice

Associated with this deadly sin are treachery, disloyalty, betrayal, and covetousness, especially when these behaviors come from a desire for personal gain. Like lust and gluttony, greed is a sin of excess. Many times it is particularly focused on money and material things. Thomas Aquinas wrote that greed is "... a sin against God, just as all mortal sins, inasmuch as man condemns things eternal for the sake of temporal things."

The following are some Bible verses that confront this sin:

"Thou shalt not covet thy neighbour's house, thou shalt not covet thy neighbour's wife, nor his manservant, nor his maidservant, nor his ox, nor his ass, nor any thing that is thy neighbour's" (Exodus 20:17).

"Lay not up for yourselves treasures upon earth, where moth and rust doth corrupt, and where thieves break through and steal: but lay up for yourselves treasures in heaven, where neither moth nor rust doth corrupt, and where thieves do not break through nor steal: for where your treasure is, there will your heart be also" (Matthew 6:19–21).

"No man can serve two masters: for either he will hate the one, and love the other; or else he will hold to the one, and despise the other. Ye cannot serve God and mammon" (Matthew 6:24).

4. Acedia—Sloth

This is the sin of laziness or indolence. It is characterized by apathy, depression, and joylessness. Often these feelings stem from attitudes of dissatisfaction and discontent. Dante wrote that sloth originates in a "... failure to love God with all one's heart, all one's mind and all one's soul." Those who are slothful fail to utilize the gifts and talents God has given to them, and they seem to not care about their responsibilities and other people.

The following verses are some Scriptures that deal with this deadly sin:

"I went by the field of the slothful, and by the vineyard of the man void of understanding; and, lo, it was all grown over with thorns, and nettles had covered the face thereof, and the stone wall thereof was broken down ... yet a little sleep, a little slumber, a little folding of the hands to sleep; so shall thy poverty come as one that travelleth; and thy want as an armed man" (Proverbs 24:30–34).

"The soul of the sluggard desireth, and hath nothing: but the soul of the diligent shall be made fat" (Proverbs 13:4).

"The slothful man saith, There is a lion in the way; a lion is in the streets. As the door turneth upon his hinges, so doth the slothful upon his bed. The slothful hideth his hand in his bosom; it grieveth him to bring it again to his mouth. The sluggard is wiser in his own conceit than seven men that can render a reason" (Proverbs 26:13–16).

5. Ira—Wrath and Intense Anger

Hatred, prejudice, and discrimination stem from this deadly sin, which involves a murderous desire for revenge. Sometimes this sin manifests as a denial of the truth, even self-denial, and great impatience in several areas of life. Wrathful persons are intolerant individuals who are self-centered and mean toward others, especially toward those who are different from themselves or those who have wronged them.

There are several Scriptures that focus on this deadly sin. Here are a couple of them:

> "Let all bitterness, and wrath, and anger, and clamour, and evil speaking, be put away from you, with all malice: and be ye kind one to another, tenderhearted, forgiving one another, even as God for Christ's sake hath forgiven you" (Ephesians 4:31–32).

> "For the wrath of man worketh not the righteousness of God. Wherefore lay apart all filthiness and superfluity of naughtiness, and receive with meekness the engrafted word, which is able to save your souls" (James 1:20–21).

6. Invidia—Envy

Envy involves resentment over what another person has or is able to do. It is accompanied with a painful desire to have the things that another possesses. It is closely associated with jealousy and malice.

The following Scriptures show how God feels about this particular deadly sin:

"A sound heart is the life of the flesh: but envy the rottenness of the bones" (Proverbs 14:30).

"Let not thine heart envy sinners: but be thou in the fear of the LORD all the day long" (Proverbs 23:17).

"Wrath is cruel, and anger is outrageous; but who is able to stand before envy?" (Proverbs 27:4).

"He is proud, knowing nothing, but doting about questions and strifes of words, whereof cometh envy, strife, railings, evil surmisings" (1 Timothy 6:4).

7. Superbia—Pride

Pride is generally considered to be the worst of the Seven Deadly Sins, because almost all sins, including the six other deadly sins, stem from pride. Pride involves vanity, hubris, and narcissism, and it represents a very unhealthy self-love that leads to selfishness in all its forms, including self-consciousness, arrogance, and conceit. People who are full of pride desire to be seen as being more important or attractive than all others. This leads to idolatry, a love of self that puts self in the place of God.

Here are some Bible verses about pride:

"Pride goeth before destruction, and an haughty spirit before a fall" (Proverbs 16:18).

"Yea, all of you be subject one to another, and be clothed with humility: for God resisteth the proud, and giveth grace to the humble. Humble yourselves therefore under the mighty hand of God, that he may exalt you in due time" (1 Peter 5:5–6).

All of the Seven Deadly Sins must be purged from a believer's life if he or she is to find the way to union with love in God, as Saint John of the Cross points out so clearly in his writings. He shows how each of us has our besetting sins that must be dealt with before we can make any spiritual progress.

Once we've gone through the various stages of the "dark night of the soul," however, we will be able to enjoy the blessings and benefits of the Seven Cardinal Virtues, which will lead us into the very heart of God and give us a wonderful sense of joy.

Before we begin our reading of *Dark Night of the Soul*, therefore, let's take a look at the Seven Cardinal Virtues, which are also known as the Seven Holy Virtues.

THE SEVEN HOLY VIRTUES

The Seven Holy Virtues are also known as the Seven Moral Virtues, the Seven Cardinal Virtues, and the Seven Theological Virtues. They are: faith, hope, love, prudence, justice, fortitude, and temperance. These serve as direct opposites to the Seven Deadly Sins.

• *Faith*—Faith involves ardent belief in God and His Word. One of the early Christian symbols for faith is a ship, which represents the Church of Jesus Christ, a vessel that carries Christians safely through life into the next life. "Now faith is the substance of things hope for, the evidence of things not seen" (Hebrews 11:1).

• *Hope*—Hope takes a positive view of the future, and it believes that the goodness of God will prevail over all forms of evil and darkness. The early Christian symbol for hope is an anchor, which contains a hidden cross.

"That by two immutable things, in which it was impossible for God to lie, we might have a strong consolation, who have fled for refuge to lay hold upon the hope set before us: which hope we have as an anchor of the soul, both sure and stedfast, and which entereth into that within the veil" (Hebrews 6:18–19).

• *Love*—Love is also known as charity. It involves loving God with all one's heart, mind, and soul; and loving and caring for others. It is symbolized by fire in the writings of Saint John of the Cross, particularly in his poem *Love's Living Flame.* "Beloved, let us love one another: for love is of God; and every one that loveth is born of God, and knoweth God. He that loveth not knoweth not God; for God is love" (1 John 4:7–8).

• *Fortitude*—Fortitude is a quality of inner strength that is reflected by an unwillingness to give up. It is perseverance and endurance in the face of all opposition. It is symbolized by a sword and shield, signifying the courage to do and to endure for God. "I can do all things through Christ which strengtheneth me" (Philippians 4:13).

• *Justice*—God is always just, and He expects us as His children to practice justice at all times. The symbol for justice is a triangle and a plumb line, both of which signify fair measures. "He hath shewed thee, O man, what is good; and what doth the LORD require of thee, but to do justly, and to love mercy, and to walk humbly with thy God" (Micah 6:8).

• *Prudence*—Prudence involves good stewardship. It takes good care of what it has been given and it manages money with God's wisdom, not human desires. It is symbolized by the serpent and the dove. Jesus said, "Behold, I send you forth as sheep in the midst of wolves: be ye therefore wise as serpents, and harmless as doves" (Matthew 10:16).

• *Temperance*—The hearth and fire symbolize temperance, the virtue by which the soul is refined through tribulations in the same way that gold is refined by fire. "But who may abide the day of his coming? and who shall stand when he appeareth? for he is like a refiner's fire, and like fuller's soap: and he shall sit as a refiner and purifier of silver: and he shall purify the sons of Levi, and purge them as gold and silver, that they may offer unto the LORD an offering in righteousness" (Malachi 3:2–3).

As you read the next work of Saint John of the Cross, his most famous work of all, you will discover the ways through which God purifies the human soul as it passes through the dark night. About this great work, Georgia Harkness has written that the *Dark Night of the Soul* "... deals with an experience which is not that of a remote time or place, or special degree of saintliness, but which besets the path of the earnest in every age. Its theme is the sense of spiritual desolation, loneliness, frustration, and despair which grips the soul of one who, having seen the vision of God and been lifted by it, finds the vision fade and the presence of God recede."

As the soul perseveres, however, it finds its way to the place of peace, tranquility, and joy—total union with its heavenly Beloved, and this is the goal that Saint John of the Cross puts forth for every seeker. His writings are as timely and relevant today as they were when this great man of God wrote them in the sixteenth century.

References

"The Seven Deadly Sins" (from Wikipedia, the Free Encyclopedia). (http://en.wikipedia.org/wiki?Seven_deadly_sins).

"The Seven Virtues" (http://changingminds.org/explanations/values/seven_virtues.htm)

Dark Night of the Soul

BY
SAINT JOHN OF THE CROSS

THE PROLOGUE

In this prologue you will find the "Stanzas of the Soul," which form the basis for *Dark Night of the Soul*. Throughout this book, the first, second, and third stanzas are discussed and expounded upon. These were the only commentaries that St. John of the Cross completed before his death.

Stanzas of the Soul

1. On a dark night, kindled in love with yearnings—
oh, happy chance!
I went forth without being observed, my house being now
at rest.

2. In darkness and secure, by the secret ladder, disguised—
oh, happy chance!
In darkness and in concealment, my house being now at
rest.

3. In the happy night, in secret, when none saw me,
Nor I beheld aught, without light or guide, save that which
burned in my heart.

4. This light guided me more surely than the light of
noonday
To the place where he (well I knew who!) was awaiting
me—
A place where none appeared.

5. Oh, night that guided me; oh, night more lovely than the
dawn,
Oh, night that joined Beloved with lover, lover transformed
in the Beloved!

6. Upon my flowery breast, kept wholly for himself alone,
There he stayed sleeping, and I caressed him, and the
fanning of the cedars made a breeze.

7. The breeze blew from the turret as I parted his locks;
With his gentle hand he wounded my neck and caused all
my senses to be suspended.

Let us now begin the exposition of the above stanzas, which reveal the way and manner by which the soul finds its way to the union of love with God.

It is well for us to understand here that the soul must travel through severe trials and tribulations in order to find this most holy, high, and happy union with God. Jesus said:

"Because strait is the gate, and narrow is the way, which leadeth unto life, and few there be that find it" (Matthew 7:14).

Since there are so few that find it, the soul considers it a great happiness and good chance to have passed along the way to the perfection of love. The first stanza of the poem speaks of this profound happiness, and it reveals that "the strait road" to which Jesus refers is the "dark night" which we must go through in order to find complete union with God.

BOOK I

THE DARK NIGHT
OF THE SENSES

The First Stanza

On a dark night, kindled in love with yearnings—
Oh, happy chance!
I went forth without being observed,
My house now at rest.

Chapter 1

THE IMPERFECTIONS OF BEGINNERS

Exposition

In this first stanza we see the soul, kindled in love and longing, going forth from itself and all other things. The soul is beginning to die to itself and other things by means of true mortification in order to attain to living the sweet and delectable life of love with God. This going forth from itself and all other things is described as a "dark night," which is a metaphor for purgative contemplation. This is what causes the soul to die to itself.

The soul is able to accomplish this "going forth" through the strength and ardor that comes from the love of its Spouse. This stanza extols the great happiness that is found in journeying to God through the dark night. None of the soul's three enemies—the devil, the world, and the flesh—are able to hinder its progress as it journeys through the night, because *"I went forth without being observed."* All the passions and desires of the soul are lulled to sleep and mortified in the dark night of purgative contemplation. Hence, "my house" is now "at rest."

"On a Dark Night"

Souls begin to enter into this dark night when God draws them forth from the state of beginners—the state of those who meditate on the spiritual road; and begins to set them in the state of the more advanced—the state of those who are already contemplatives. The goal is that, after passing through these states, they would be able to arrive at the state of the perfect—divine union of the soul with God.

In order to understand this dark night better, let's take a look at certain characteristics of beginners so that, realizing the weak state they are in, they may take courage and desire that God will bring them into this dark night through which the soul is strengthened, confirmed in the virtues, and made ready for the inestimable delights of the love of God.

Pleasure in Spiritual Exercises

The soul, after it has been definitely converted to the service of God is, as a rule, spiritually nurtured and caressed by God in much the same way that a loving mother caresses her tender child and warms it with the heat of her bosom and nurtures it with sweet milk and soft, pleasant food. The mother carries and caresses her child in her arms. Then, as the child grows bigger, she gradually stops the caressing and, hiding her tender love, puts bitter aloes upon her sweet breast and sets the child down, making it learn to walk upon its own feet, so that it may lose the habits of a child and go on to more important things.

The loving mother is like the grace of God, for, as soon as the soul is regenerated by its new warmth and fervor for

84

the service of God, He treats it in the same way that the mother treats her child. He makes it find sweet and delectable spiritual milk in all the things of God without any labor of its own. The soul then finds great pleasure in spiritual exercises, for God is giving it the breast of His tender love in the same way that a mother does with her child.

Imperfect Striving

Therefore, such a soul finds its delight in spending long periods—perhaps even whole nights—in prayer. Penances become its pleasures and fasts become its joys. Its consolations are found in the sacraments and in being occupied with divine things. Spiritual persons may find themselves to be very weak and imperfect as they take part in these divine things even though they do so with great efficacy, persistence, and care.

However, since they are moved to these things and to these spiritual exercises by the consolation and pleasure they find in them, and since they have not been prepared for them by the practice of earnest striving in the virtues, they may find they have many faults and imperfections. It is wise to remember here that a person's actions correspond to the degree of perfection that he or she has attained to, as a habit, with regard to those actions.

Because these people have not had the opportunity of acquiring habits of strength, they find themselves having to work somewhat feebly, like children. In order to make this more clearly understandable we shall take a look at the seven capital sins and the various imperfections they bring about in a person's life. This will help us to see how the beginner is very much like a child in many respects, and it will also help us to see the many blessings the dark night of the soul provides for us, since it cleanses the soul and purifies it from all imperfections.

Chapter 2

SPIRITUAL IMPERFECTIONS WHICH BEGINNERS HAVE WITH RESPECT TO PRIDE

A Secret Pride

As these beginners begin to feel that they are being very fervent and diligent in spiritual things and devout exercises, there often comes to them, as a result of their imperfections, a certain kind of secret pride. (This happens in spite of the fact that holy things by their very nature cause humility.) This secret pride comes to them from the degree of satisfaction they may feel with regard to their works and themselves.

Hence, a certain vain desire comes to them, a desire to speak of spiritual things in the presence of others. They may even strive to teach such things rather than being content with simply learning them. In so doing, they may condemn others within their hearts when they see that others may not have the kind of devotion that they themselves desire. Sometimes they will even utter these judgments aloud like the Pharisee who boasted by praising God for his own good works and despising the publican:

> The Pharisee stood and prayed thus with himself, God, I thank thee, that I am not as other men are, extortioners, unjust, adulterers, or even as this publican. I fast twice in the week, I give tithes of all that I possess (Luke 18:11–12).

Temptations of the Evil One

The devil often influences these persons to increase their fervor and their desire to perform these works more frequently. In this way he is able to ensure that their pride and presumption will grow greater. The devil knows quite well that all these works they perform are not only valueless to them, but they even become vices within them. Evil enters the picture when these persons think that they are the only ones who are good or appear to be good and when they don't want anyone else to appear to be good. Thus, in both deed and word they condemn and slander others. These are the ones Jesus describes in the following verses:

And why beholdest thou the mote that is in thy brother's eye, but considerest not the beam that is in thine own eye? (Matthew 7:3)

Ye blind guides, which strain at a gnat, and swallow a camel (Matthew 23:24).

Seeking the Esteem and Praise of Others

Whenever their spiritual leaders, such as pastors and teachers, do not approve of their spirit and behavior, because they know they are eager to be esteemed and praised, these persons feel that they are not being understood. As a result, they will oftentimes think that their leaders are not spiritual enough. When this happens, they look for others who will approve of them and their behavior, those who will praise them and esteem them for what they do. In so doing, they literally flee from those who disabuse them or try to guide them to a safer road. Frequently they will even feel ill will toward such leaders.

These people usually accomplish very little, because they are so eager to have others realize how spiritual and devout they are. They endeavor to exhibit these qualities through spiritual movements, signs, and ceremonies. Sometimes in public they will even fall into ecstasies which are aided by the devil. Their only concern is to be noticed by others, and their desire to be noticed drives them increasingly to outward displays.

A False Confession

Many such persons desire to be their confessors' favorites and to become intimate with them. This often leads them into envy and restlessness. They are too embarrassed to confess their sins openly, because they don't want their confessors to think less of them. Therefore, they palliate their confessors in order to excuse themselves rather than to accuse themselves by confessing their sins.

Sometimes they will find another person to whom they will confess their actual sins. In this way their own spiritual leader will continue to think that they have done nothing wrong at all. They want their leaders/mentors to think that they do only good; thus, they take great pleasure in telling them about their goodness and good deeds, usually in terms that make their goodness seem greater than it actually is. Their obvious desire is that they would think of them as being good. They don't realize that it would be a sign of greater humility in them if they were to depreciate their goodness and desire that others would regard them as being less good.

Anger and Impatience

Some of these beginners make little of their faults and often become very sad when they see themselves fall into faults and errors, because they have presumed that they were already perfect. Thus, they become very angry and impatient with themselves, and this is another imperfection in their lives.

Often they will beseech God with great yearnings, and they will ask Him to take away their imperfections and faults. They do not do this for God's sake, but simply because they want to be untroubled and have peace. They do not realize that if He were to take away these faults and imperfections, they might grow prouder and more presumptuous. These people do not like to praise others, but they love to be praised, and sometimes they will even seek out such praise. They are like the foolish virgins who, when their lamps could not be lit, sought oil from others:

> And the foolish said unto the wise, Give us of your oil; for our lamps are gone out (Matthew 25:8).

Humility

From these imperfections some souls go on to develop graver ones, which do them great harm. However, while some develop greater imperfections, others begin to grow and have fewer imperfections. Those who are going on to perfection proceed very differently than the former group, with a different spiritual temperament. They progress by means of humility and are greatly edified. They think little of their own affairs, and they have very little satisfaction with themselves. They consider others as better than themselves and usually have a holy envy of them. They are eager to serve God.

Their fervor in serving Him is great, and they take great pleasure in doing so. As they progress in humility, they realize more and more how much they owe to God and how little they actually do for Him. Thus, the more they do, the less they are satisfied. They would gladly do so much out of charity and love for Him that what they do seems to be almost nothing to them. So greatly are they importuned, occupied, and absorbed by this loving anxiety that they never notice what others do or don't do or, if they do notice what others do or don't do, they always believe that the others are far better than they are.

They regard themselves as being of little worth and they want others to see them as such, and they hope that others will despise and depreciate what they do. Further, if others should praise and esteem them, they do not believe what they say. In fact, it seems strange to them that others would even say good things about them.

A Teachable Spirit

Together with great tranquility and humility, these souls have a deep desire to be taught by anyone who can help them. They are the complete opposite of those we referred to earlier, those who prefer to teach rather than to be taught. When others are teaching this latter group, they take the words from their teachers' mouths as if they knew them already.

These more teachable souls, on the other hand, being far from desiring to be the masters of others, are always ready to travel and change the course of their direction, if their teachers command them to do so, because they know they need their teachers' guidance. These souls rejoice when others are praised, and they grieve because they cannot serve God as others do. They have no desire to speak of the things that they do, because they think so little of them that they are ashamed to speak of them even to their spiritual leaders and teachers.

They think that what they do does not deserve to be spoken of. They are more eager to speak of their own faults and sins, so that these, rather than their virtues, would be recognized. Thus, they are inclined to talk about the issues of their souls with those who view their actions and their spirituality as being of little value. These are the characteristics of those whose spirits are simple, pure, genuine, and very pleasing to God. For, as the wise Spirit of God dwells in these humble souls, He moves them and inclines them to keep His treasures secretly within and, likewise, to cast all evil from their lives. God gives this grace to the humble along with all the other virtues, but He denies them to the proud.

God Leads Them into the Dark Night

These souls will give their heart's blood to anyone who serves God, and they will help others to serve Him in whatever ways they can. They bear the imperfections into which they fall with humility, meekness of spirit, a loving fear of God, and hope in Him. But these souls comprise a minority. God leads those He desires to purify from all imperfections into the dark night so that He may lead them onward.

Chapter 3

SPIRITUAL IMPERFECTIONS WHICH BEGINNERS HAVE WITH RESPECT TO AVARICE OR GREED

Spiritual Avarice

Most of these beginners experience great spiritual avarice at times. They are discontented with the spirituality God gives to them, and they are very disconsolate and querulous because they do not find the consolation they desire in spiritual things. Many can never have enough of listening to counsel and learning spiritual precepts and of possessing and reading many books which deal with these important matters. They often spend their time on these things rather than on works of mortification and the perfection of their inward poverty of spirit, which they should desire.

Furthermore, they burden themselves with images and rosaries which are very curious. They put one down; then they take up another. They are very changeable. They prefer one kind of cross to another. They adorn themselves with various medals, relics, and tokens, as children do with trinkets.

Here I condemn the attachment of the heart and the affection and curiosity they have for the nature and multitude of these things, because such attachment is quite contrary to the poverty of spirit that considers only the substance of devotion, makes use only of what suffices for that end, and grows weary of any other kind of multiplicity and curiosity.

True devotion must issue from the heart, and it must consist alone in the truth and substance of what is represented by spiritual things; all the rest is affection and attachment that proceed from imperfection. In order for one to pass to any kind of perfection it is necessary for all such desires to be killed.

Being Right with God

I knew a person who for more than ten years made use of a cross that had been roughly formed from a branch, perhaps an olive or rosemary branch that was blessed in a church on Palm Sunday. This cross was fastened with a pin that was twisted around it. He never ceased using it, and he always carried it with him until I took it from him. He was a person of no small intellect and understanding.

I knew someone else who said his prayers using beads that were made of bones from the spine of a fish. His devotion was certainly no less precious on that account in the sight of God, for it is clear that these things carried no devotion in their workmanship or value.

Those, then, who start from these beginnings and make good progress, attach themselves to no visible instruments, and they do not burden themselves with such, nor desire to know more than is necessary in order to act well. They set their eyes only on being right with God and pleasing Him. Therein their covetousness consists. Therefore, with great generosity they give away all that they have and delight to know that they no longer have it for God's sake and for charity to their neighbors, no matter whether these things be spiritual or temporal. They set their eyes only upon the reality of interior perfection, which is to give pleasure to God and not to give pleasure to them.

The Passive Purgation of That Dark Night

From these various imperfections the soul cannot be perfectly purified until God brings it into the passive purgation of the dark night. It befits the soul, however, to contrive to labor, insofar as it can, on its own account, to the end that it may purge and perfect itself, and thus may merit being taken by God into that divine care in which it becomes healed of all things that it was unable of itself to cure.

However greatly the soul itself labors, it cannot actively purify itself so as to be in the least degree prepared for the divine union of perfect love, if God does not take its hand and purge it in that dark fire, in the manner and way that we shall describe.

Chapter 4

SPIRITUAL IMPERFECTIONS WHICH BEGINNERS HAVE WITH RESPECT TO LUXURY

Impure Acts and Motions

Many beginners have several other imperfections besides those which I am describing with respect to each of the Seven Deadly Sins. I am touching on only those that seem to be the most important, because these are usually the origin and cause of the rest. Thus, with respect to the sin of luxury (a sin that must be purged by the dark night), we need to mention the sin of spiritual luxury, because its imperfections proceed from spiritual things.

In their spiritual exercises these beginners are powerless to prevent such spiritual luxuries in their lives, because certain impure acts and motions arise and assert themselves in the sensual part of their souls, sometimes even when they are in prayer or engaged in the various sacraments. These things are not within their power to control; they proceed from three causes, which I delineate in the following paragraphs.

Pleasure in Spiritual Things

The first of these causes is the pleasure which human nature takes in spiritual things. When the spirit and the senses are pleased, every part of the person is moved by that pleasure and delights in it according to its proportion and nature. When the spirit, which is the highest part of a person's makeup, is moved to pleasure and takes delight in God, and the sensual nature, which is the lowest part of a person's makeup, is moved to pleasure and delight of the senses, because it cannot possess and lay hold upon anything else, it lays hold upon that which comes nearest to itself—the impure and the sensual.

Thus, it comes to pass that the soul is in deep prayer with God according to the spirit; on the other hand, according to sense, it is passively conscious, not without great displeasure, of rebellions and motions and acts of the senses, which often happens during Communion. When the soul receives joy and comfort in this act of love, because the Lord bestows it (since it is to that end that He gives himself), the sensual nature takes that which is its own, as we have said, after its manner.

Now as these two parts are combined in one individual, they ordinarily both participate in that which one of them receives, each after its manner; for, as the philosopher says, everything that is received is in the recipient after the manner of the same recipient. And thus in these beginnings, even when the soul has made some progress, its sensual part, being imperfect, oftentimes receives the Spirit of God with the same imperfection. When the sensual part is renewed by the purgation of the dark night, which we shall describe, it no longer has these weaknesses, for it is no longer this part that receives anything, but it is itself received into the spirit. Thus, it then has everything after the manner of the spirit.

94

The Devil Stirs Up Motions of Impurity

The second cause from which these rebellions sometimes proceed is the devil, who, in order to trouble and disturb the soul when it is at prayer or is striving to pray, contrives to stir up motions of impurity in the very nature of the soul. If the soul gives heed to any of these temptations, they will cause great harm.

Through fear of these things people will become lax in prayer, and this is the devil's aim as he begins to strive with them. This leads some to give up prayer altogether, because they think that these things attack them more during prayer than at other times. This may cause them to give up spiritual exercises altogether.

The devil then proceeds to vividly portray to them things that are most foul and impure. Oftentimes these things are related to certain spiritual things and persons that are of profit to their souls. This temptation terrifies them and makes them fearful, and causes them to ignore spiritual things, because of the temptations they encounter when praying or engaging in any spiritual acts.

Those who are inclined to depression or melancholy are especially affected by this. They become greatly to be pitied because they suffer so sadly. Such people may feel that the devil is always present with them and they have no power against him, although some of these people are able to keep him at bay through hard work and great effort. When these impurities attack such souls through depression and melancholy, they are usually not freed from them until they have been cured through the dark night of the soul. This is what will rid them of all impurities.

Fear

The third source from which these impure motions are apt to proceed in order to make war upon the soul is often the fear which such persons have related to these impure representations and motions. Something they see, say, or think will bring these impurities to their minds, and this makes them afraid, causing them to suffer from them through no fault of their own.

The Role of the Emotions

There are also certain souls who are of so tender and frail a nature that, when some spiritual grace or consolation comes to them in prayer, the spirit of luxury emerges immediately, causing them to become inebriated and delighted by their sensual nature in such a manner that it is as if they are plunged into the enjoyment and pleasure of this sin. The enjoyment, along with the consolation, remains with them passively, and sometimes they are able to see that certain impure and unruly acts have taken place. The reason for this is that since their natures are so frail and tender, their emotions are stirred up and excited by the least disturbance. The same thing happens to such souls when they feel angry or suffer any kind of disturbance or grief.

Vain Gratification and Complacency in the Will

Sometimes there arises within these spiritual persons, whether they be speaking or performing spiritual actions, a certain vigor and bravado through their having regard to persons who are present. Before these persons they display a certain kind of vain gratification. This also arises from luxury of the spirit, which is accompanied as a rule by complacency in the will.

Friendships and Two Kinds of Love

Some of these persons make friendships of a spiritual kind with others, which oftentimes arise from luxury and not from spirituality. This is the case when the remembrance of that friendship causes not the remembrance and love of

God to grow, but causes remorse of conscience. For when the friendship is purely spiritual, the love of God grows with it, and the more the soul remembers it. When this happens, the more it remembers the love of God, the greater is its desire for God. As one grows, therefore, the other grows as well. The Spirit of God has this property—it increases good by adding to it more good.

However, when this loves arises from the vice of sensuality, it produces the contrary effects. The more the one grows, the more the other decreases, and the remembrance of it decreases likewise. If that sensual love grows, it will at once be observed that the soul's love of God will become colder, forgetting Him as it remembers that love. This brings about a certain remorse of conscience.

On the other hand, if the love of God grows in the soul, the other kind of love becomes cold and forgotten, for the two are contrary one to another. The one does not aid the other, but the one which predominates quenches and confounds the other and becomes strengthened in itself.

Our Savior makes this quite clear: "That which is born of the flesh is flesh; and that which is born of the Spirit is spirit" (John 3:6). That is to say that the love which is born of sensuality ends in sensuality, and the love which is born of the Spirit ends in the Spirit of God, who causes it to keep on growing. This is the difference that exists between these two kinds of love.

Strengthening the Love of God

When the soul enters the dark night, it brings the two kinds of love under control. It strengthens and purifies the one (the love of God), and it removes and brings to an end sensual love. At first, however, it causes the soul to lose sight of both.

Chapter 5

SPIRITUAL IMPERFECTIONS WHICH BEGINNERS HAVE WITH RESPECT TO THE SIN OF WRATH

Bitterness and Anger

By reason of the strong desire which many beginners have for spiritual consolations, their experience of these consolations is very commonly accompanied by many imperfections proceeding from the sin of wrath; for, when their delight and pleasure in spiritual things come to an end, they naturally become embittered and show forth that lack of sweetness which they have to suffer with a bad grace. This affects all that they do, and they become irritated over the smallest matter to the point that no one can even tolerate them.

This frequently happens after they have been very pleasantly recollected in prayer according to sense. When their pleasure and delight in prayer come to an end, their nature becomes vexed and disappointed in the same way that a child grows upset when it is taken from its mother's breast, where it was enjoying comfort and sweetness. There is no sin in this natural vexation when it is permitted to indulge itself, but there is imperfection which must be purged by the aridity and severity of the dark night.

Irritation at the Sins of Others

There are other persons who fall into another kind of spiritual wrath—irritation at the sins of others. This happens when they keep watch on others with an uneasy zeal. At times the impulse comes to them to reprove others angrily. Sometimes they nurture and cultivate this anger by setting themselves up as masters of virtue. All this, of course, is contrary to spiritual meekness.

Impatience with One's Own Imperfections

There are others who become vexed with themselves when they observe their own imperfections. When this happens, they display an impatience that is unlike humility. They grow very impatient about it, as if they were trying to become saints in a day. Many of these persons purpose to accomplish a great deal, and they make grand resolutions. Yet, as they are not humble and have no misgivings about themselves, the more resolutions they make, and the greater is their fall and their annoyance. This happens because they do not have the patience to wait for that which God will give to them when it pleases Him to do so. This likewise is contrary to the spiritual meekness mentioned above, and it cannot be remedied except through the purgation that is provided by the dark night of the soul.

Chapter 6

SPIRITUAL IMPERFECTIONS WHICH BEGINNERS HAVE WITH RESPECT TO GLUTTONY

Spiritual Gluttony

With respect to the fourth sin, spiritual gluttony, there is much to be said, for there are hardly any beginners who, however satisfactory their progress, do not fall into some of the many imperfections related to this sin. This happens as a result of the sweetness they find at first in spiritual exercises. For many of them, lured by the sweetness and pleasure they find in such exercises, begin to strive more after the sweetness rather than the spiritual purity and discretion that God desires and accepts throughout one's spiritual journey.

Therefore, besides the imperfections into which the seeking for sweetness makes them fall, the spiritual gluttony which they now have makes them continually go to extremes, so much so that they pass beyond the limits of moderation within which the virtues are acquired and have their being. Some of these persons are attracted by the pleasure which they find therein, and they kill themselves with penances; while others weaken themselves through fasts and by performing beyond what their weakness can bear. They avoid the advice of others whom they should be obeying with regard to such matters. Indeed, some will even launch out on their own, even though they've been commanded not to do so.

Disobedience and Its Results

These persons are most imperfect and unreasonable. They set bodily penance before subjection and obedience, which lead to penance according to reason and discretion—a sacrifice which is more acceptable and pleasing to God than any other. Such one-sided penance is no more than the penance of beasts. Like beasts, they are attracted by the desire and pleasure they find therein.

Inasmuch as all extremes are vicious and inasmuch as such persons are working their own will in disobedience, they grow in vice rather than in virtue. They are acquiring spiritual gluttony and pride in this way—by walking in disobedience. The devil assails many of these persons by stirring up gluttony in them through the pleasures and desires which he continually increases in them. He does this to such an extent that, since they can no longer help themselves, they either change or vary or add to that which is commanded to them, because obedience is so bitter to them. Many of these people enter into a degree of evil that prevents them from obedience altogether, and they lose the desire and devotion to obey, because their only desire and pleasure is to do what they are inclined to do. Therefore, it would be more profitable for them not to engage in spiritual exercises at all.

Clinging to Their Own Will and Pleasure

Many of these persons are very insistent with their spiritual mentors by demanding that they grant their desires. They become so insistent that they try to extract what they want from their spiritual masters almost by force. If they are refused, they become as peevish as children who do not get their own way, and they go about in great displeasure, thinking that they are not serving God when they are not allowed to do what they want to do.

Boldness and Temerity

There are others who, because of this gluttony, know very little of their own unworthiness and misery. They have thrust the loving fear and reverence of God far from themselves. They do not hesitate to insist continually that their confessors shall allow them to communicate with them very frequently. What is worse, they frequently dare to communicate with their pastors, teachers, and confessors—the ministers and stewards of Christ—even without their permission and consent. Instead, they merely act on their own opinions and even contrive to conceal the truth from those who are in authority over them.

For this reason, because they desire such constant communication with their ministers, they make their confessions carelessly, because they are more eager to eat than they are to eat cleanly and perfectly. Obviously, it would be healthier and holier for them to have the contrary inclination by begging their leaders not to command them to approach the altar so frequently. Between these two extremes, however, is the better way of humble resignation. The boldness of these persons, though, is a thing that does great harm and such people should fear punishment for such temerity.

101

Impurity in Faith

These persons, in all their communicating, strive with all their nerves to obtain some kind of sensible sweetness and pleasure instead of humbly doing reverence and giving praise within themselves to God. When they have received no pleasure or sweetness in their senses, they think they have accomplished nothing at all. In so doing they are judging God very unworthily, for they have failed to realize that the least of the benefits that come from this sacrament is that which concerns the senses. The invisible part of the grace that it bestows is much greater than anything related to the senses. In order that they may look at it with the eyes of faith, God often withholds from them these other consolations and the sweetness of sense. They desire to feel and taste God, as though He were comprehensible by them and accessible to them not only in this, but likewise in all other spiritual practices. All this is very great imperfection, and is completely opposed to the nature of God, because it is impurity in faith.

The Loss of True Devotion and Spirituality

These persons have the same defect when it comes to the practice of prayer, for they think that prayer consists in experiencing sensual pleasure, which they strive to obtain by great effort. They weary and fatigue their faculties and their heads. When they do not find this pleasure, they become greatly discouraged, thinking that they have accomplished nothing.

Through these efforts they lose true devotion and spirituality, which consist of perseverance, patience, humility, and distrust of themselves, that they may please God alone. For this reason, when they fail to find pleasure in this or any other exercise, they are reluctant to return to it and may even find it repugnant. Therefore, they sometimes go so far as to abandon it altogether.

They are like children who are not influenced by reason and don't act from rational motives; instead, they are moved by pleasure. Such persons expend all their effort in seeking spiritual pleasure and consolation. They never tire, therefore, of reading books, and they go from one thing to the next in their pursuit of pleasure, which they desire to experience in the things of God.

But God, very justly, wisely, and lovingly, denies such pleasure to them. Otherwise, the spiritual gluttony and inordinate appetite would breed innumerable evils. It is therefore very fitting that they should enter into the dark night, that they may be purged from their childishness.

Self-Denial Is Devoid of Sweetness

The persons who are inclined to such pleasures have another very great imperfection, which is that they are very weak, and they are remiss when it comes to journeying along the hard road of the cross. The soul that is given to sweetness naturally has its face set against all self-denial, which is devoid of sweetness.

The Results of Spiritual Temperance and Sobriety

These persons have many other imperfections as well. In time the Lord heals them of these by means of temptations, dry spells, and other trials, all of which are part of the dark night. Spiritual temperance and sobriety lead to another, very different temper, which is that of mortification, fear, and submission in all things.

It thus becomes clear that the perfection and worth of things consists not in the multitude and the pleasantness of one's actions, but in being able to deny oneself in them. This is what these persons must strive for insofar as they are able to do so, until God is pleased to purify them indeed by bringing them into the dark night.

Chapter 7

SPIRITUAL IMPERFECTIONS WHICH BEGINNERS HAVE WITH RESPECT TO ENVY AND SLOTH

Love Does Not Envy

Spiritual envy and sloth are two other vices which beginners often struggle with. With respect to envy, many of these people will experience moments of displeasure at the spiritual good of others. This causes them to be outstripped along the way, and they would rather not hear others being praised. They become displeased by others' virtues and will often not refrain from contradicting what may be said in praise of others, and will even depreciate it as much as they can, because the same is not said of them. They want to be preferred in everything.

All this of course is contrary to love and charity. St. Paul writes, "Charity ... rejoiceth not in iniquity, but rejoiceth in the truth" (1 Corinthians 13:6). Yes, true charity rejoices in goodness, and if it has any envy at all, it is a holy envy, which comprises grief over the realization that one does not have the same virtues another has. At the same time, however, it experiences joy over the fact that others do have those virtues and takes delight when others do well in the service of God.

Abandoning the Way of Perfection

With respect to spiritual sloth, beginners are apt to be irked by the things that are most spiritual, and may even flee from them because such things are incompatible with the pleasures of the senses. Because they are so accustomed to sweetness in spiritual things, they grow weary by things in which they find no sweetness. For example, if they failed to find the satisfaction their tastes required in prayer (and, after all, it is well that God should take it from them in order to prove them), they would usually prefer not to return to it. Sometimes, therefore, they leave it altogether, or they may continue in it reluctantly and unwillingly. Thus, because of this spiritual sloth, they abandon the way of perfection (the way of the negation of their will and pleasure for God's sake) in order to return to the pleasure and sweetness of their own will, which they aim to satisfy rather than finding their satisfaction in the will of God.

The Battle of Two Wills

Many of these would like to have God will the same things they will, and they are fretful over having to conform their wills to His. In truth, they find it repugnant to accommodate their wills to the will of God. They want their sense of pleasure to be the will of God and they think that God is satisfied when they are satisfied. Thus, they measure God by themselves rather than measuring themselves by God, and this causes them to act in a way that is contrary to the message of the Gospel of Jesus Christ:

> "For whosoever will save his life shall lose it: and whosoever will lose his life for my sake shall find it" (Matthew 16:25).

Bearing the Trials of Perfection

These persons find it irksome when they are commanded to do that wherein they can take or find no pleasure. This is because they aim at spiritual sweetness and consolation, and they are too weak to have the fortitude required to bear the trials of perfection. They resemble those who are softly nurtured and who fretfully run away from anything that is difficult. Likewise, they take offense at the Cross, wherein all the delights of the spirit are found. The more spiritual a thing is, the more irksome it becomes to them, for as they seek to go about spiritual matters with a complete sense of freedom and according to the inclination of their wills, it causes them great sorrow and repugnance to enter upon the narrow way which, says Christ, is the way of life: "Enter ye in at the strait gate: for wide is the gate, and broad is the way, that leadeth to destruction, and many there be which go in thereat" (Matthew 7:13).

The Purgation of the Dark Night

The imperfections which we have been discussing are often found in the lives of those who are in the first stage of beginners. They serve to show us how greatly these people need God to lead them to become proficient in the spiritual life. He does this by bringing them into the dark night of the soul, wherein He weans them from the breasts of the sweetness and pleasures they have long sought and gives them dry spells and inward darkness in order to remove from them all irrelevancies and weaknesses so that they will obtain the virtues He desires for them.

However assiduously the beginners attempt to practice the mortification of the flesh within themselves through various actions and passions, they can never completely succeed in doing so—far from it, in fact—until God works it into them passively by means of the dark night. May God then be pleased to give me His divine light, because this is what is needed in a night that is so dark and a matter that is too difficult to adequately describe. The line to remain focused on, therefore, is: *In a dark night.*

Chapter 8

THE EXPOUNDING OF THE FIRST STANZA— AN EXPLANATION OF THIS DARK NIGHT

Contemplation

This dark night is contemplation, and it produces in spiritual persons two kinds of darkness or purgation. These two kinds correspond to the two parts of human nature; namely, the sensual and the spiritual. Thus, one night or purgation will be sensual, wherein the soul is purged according to sense, which is subdued to the spirit. The other is a night or purgation which is spiritual, wherein the soul is purged and stripped according to the spirit, and it is subdued and made ready for the union of love with God. The night of sense is common and it comes to many beginners, and we shall speak of it first. The night of the spirit, on the other hand, is the portion of very few—those who are already practiced and proficient in the spiritual life.

The Night of Sense

The first purgation or night is bitter and terrible to the senses, as we shall now show. The second bears no comparison with it, for it is horrible and awful to the spirit, as we shall show presently. Since the night of the sense is first in order, we shall first of all say something about it briefly. More will be discussed about it later. Now we shall proceed to discuss the spiritual night more fully, since very little is said about it either in speech or in writing, and very little is known of it even by experience.

God Desires to Lead Us Farther

Since the conduct of these beginners upon the way of God is ignoble or low, and since it has much to do with their love of self and their own inclinations, as has already been explained, it's important to point out that God desires to lead them farther. He seeks to bring them out of that ignoble kind of love to a higher degree of love for Him, to free them from the ignoble exercises of sense and the wrong kind of meditation. By this kind of meditation we mean that they use it to go seeking God in an unworthy manner and in unbefitting ways. God wants to lead them to a kind of spiritual exercise wherein they can commune with Him more abundantly and are freed more completely from all imperfections.

For some time now they have had some practice in the way of virtue and they have persevered in meditation and prayer, in which, by the sweetness and pleasure they have found therein, they have lost their love of the things of the world and have gained some degree of spiritual strength in God. This has to some extent enabled them to refrain from creature desires, so that for God's sake they are now able to suffer a light burden and dryness without turning back to a time when they found more pleasant things in life.

When they go about these spiritual exercises with the greatest delight and pleasure, and when they believe that the sun of divine favor is shining most brightly upon them, God turns all this light of theirs into darkness and shuts against them the door and the source of the sweet spiritual water they were tasting in Him for as long as they desired and whenever they desired it. (For, as they were weak and tender, there was no door closed to them.)

Thus God leaves them so completely in the dark that they do not know where to go with their imagination and meditation, for they cannot advance a step in meditation as they once did, because their senses are submerged in the dark night; and they are left with such a dryness that the pleasure and consolation they used to experience is absorbed by a lack of taste and bitterness instead.

God now sees that they have grown a bit and are becoming strong enough to lay aside their "swaddling clothes" and be taken from the gentle breast. Therefore, He sets them down from His arms and teaches them to walk on their own two feet. This is very strange for them, for they feel that everything seems to be going wrong.

The Blessed Night

This commonly happens to some soon after their beginnings. Others, however, have to go through a longer process. The ones who are making the best progress are those who are freer from occasions of backsliding, and their desires turn more quickly away from the things of the world. This of course is necessary if they are to begin to enter the blessed night of sense. Ordinarily no great time passes after their beginnings before they begin to enter this night of sense, and the great majority of them do in fact enter it, for they will generally fall into arid and dry spells.

The Role of the Scriptures

With regard to this way of purgation of the senses, since it is so common we might here add a great number of quotations from the Holy Scriptures, which contain many passages related to this important subject. Many of these passages are found in the Psalms and the Prophets, but we will not quote them here, because we realize that those who know how to use the Bible will be able to find them for themselves. The ones who do not know how to look for the appropriate Scriptures will find the experience of purgation to be sufficient at this time.

Chapter 9

THE SIGNS THAT SHOW THAT A SPIRITUAL PERSON IS WALKING ALONG THE WAY OF THIS DARK NIGHT AND IS THEREBY BEING PURGED OF THE SENSES

Three Principal Signs

The dry spells that a beginner experiences might frequently proceed, not from the night and purgation of the sensual desires, but from sins and imperfections, from weaknesses and being lukewarm, or perhaps from physical illnesses. In this chapter I will set down certain signs by which it may be known if the dry spells proceed from the aforementioned purgation or from the sins and conditions I list above. There are three principal signs that help us to know, and these are discussed fully in the following paragraphs.

The Things of God

The first of these signs relates to whether a soul finds pleasure or consolation in the things of God and fails to find pleasure and consolation in created things. As God sets the soul in this dark night, He does so in order to quench and purge all sensual desires from the soul. He will not permit the soul to find attraction or sweetness in anything this world has to offer. In this case the dryness that a soul experiences probably does not proceed from recently committed sins or imperfections, for, if this were so, the soul would feel in its nature some inclination or desire to taste things other than the things of God.

Whenever desire is allowed indulgence in any imperfection, it immediately feels drawn to it, whether little or much, in proportion to the pleasure and love the soul has put into it.

110

However, since this lack of enjoyment in things above or even in things below might proceed from illness or depression, it becomes necessary to apply the second sign and condition.

Dryness and Being Lukewarm

The second sign whereby individuals may believe themselves to be in the experience of the said purgation is that their memory is ordinarily centered upon God with painful care and solicitude, thinking that it is not serving God, but is backsliding, because it finds itself without sweetness in the things of God. In such a case it is evident that this lack of sweetness and related dryness do not come from weakness and being lukewarm, because it is the nature of being lukewarm not to care greatly or to have any inward solicitude for the things of God.

There is a great difference between dryness and being lukewarm, for being lukewarm consists in great weakness of the will and of the spirit, without solicitude with regard to serving God. On the other hand, the dryness that comes from purgation is ordinarily accompanied by attentive care and grief, because the soul is not serving God. Although this may sometimes be increased by depression or some other negative aspect, it does not fail for that reason to produce a purgative effect upon the desire, since the desire is deprived of all pleasure and has its care centered upon God alone.

For, when certain mind-sets such as depression are the cause, the soul spends itself in displeasure and the ruin of the physical nature, and there are none of those desires to sense God which belong to purgative dryness. When the cause is aridity, it is true that the sensual part of the soul has fallen low and is weak and feeble in its actions by reason of the little pleasure which it finds in them; but the spirit, on the other hand, is ready and strong.

The Soul and the Spirit

The cause of this dryness is that God transfers to the spirit the good things and the strength of the senses, which, since the soul's natural strength and senses are incapable of using them, remain barren, dry, and empty. This happens because the sensual part of a person has no capacity for that which is pure spirit; thus, when it is the spirit that receives the pleasure, the flesh is left without savor and is too weak to perform any action.

But the spirit, which all the time is being fed, goes forward in strength, and with more alertness and solicitude than before in its anxiety not to fail God. If it is not immediately conscious of spiritual sweetness and delight, but only of dryness and a lack of sweetness, the reason is found in the strangeness of the exchange, for its palate has been accustomed to those other sensual pleasures upon which its eyes are still fixed; and since the spiritual palate is not made ready or purged from such subtle pleasure until it finds itself becoming prepared for it by means of this dark and arid night, it cannot experience spiritual pleasure and good, but only dryness and lack of sweetness, since it misses the pleasure it had previously enjoyed.

Like the Children of Israel

These souls whom God is beginning to lead through the solitary places of the wilderness are like the children of Israel, to whom God gave food from Heaven while they were in the wilderness. This manna contained sweetness, and the people began to savor it. Before long, however, the children of Israel felt the lack of the pleasures and delights of the flesh that had been provided by the onions of Egypt. Their palates were accustomed to the Egyptian food and they had taken great delight in it. Therefore, the angelic manna began to lose its appeal, and so they wept, complained, and sighed for the fleshpots of Egypt even though food from Heaven had been provided for them. To such depths does the vileness of our desires descend that they make us long for our own wretched food and be nauseated by the blessings of Heaven!

Solitude and Quietness

When the dry spells proceed from the purgation of sensual desire, although at first the spirit will feel no sweetness, it feels that it is deriving strength and energy to act from the substance which this inward spiritual food provides. This food is the beginning of contemplation, which is dark and arid to the senses. Often it is even hidden from the person who is experiencing it, and ordinarily, together with the dryness and emptiness which it causes in the senses, it gives the soul an inclination and desire to be alone and in quietness, without being able to think of any particular thing or having the desire to do so.

If those souls to whom this comes to pass knew how to be quiet at this time and not too troubled about performing any kind of action, whether inward or outward, and had no anxiety about doing anything, they would delicately experience this inward refreshment that is found in ease and freedom from care. So delicate is this refreshment that ordinarily, if they have desire or care to experience it, they will not experience it. It does its work when the soul is most at ease and free from care. It is like the air which, if anyone would close their hand upon it, escapes from their grasp.

God Is Working in the Soul

Let's take a look at what the spouse said to the Bride in the Song of Solomon: "Turn away thine eyes from me, for they have overcome me" (Song of Solomon 6:5). The phrase "... for they have overcome me" can also be translated as "... for they make me to soar aloft." It is in this way that God brings the soul out of the dry spells of the night of the senses and draws it from the life of the senses into that of the spirit. The soul goes from meditation to contemplation, and in this state it no longer has any power to work or to reason with its faculties concerning the things of God.

It is God who is now working in the soul. He binds its interior faculties and does not allow it to cling to the understanding nor have delight in the will. Nor does He allow it to reason with the memory. Anything that the soul can do of its own accord at this time serves only to hinder inward peace and the work which God is accomplishing in the spirit by means of dryness of sense. This peace is both delicate and spiritual, and it performs a work that is quiet, delicate, solitary, and productive of peace and satisfaction. It is far removed from all earlier pleasures, which were very palpable and sensual. This is the peace that David refers to in the Psalms: "I will hear what God the LORD will speak: for he will speak peace unto his people, and to his saints: but let them not turn again to folly" (Psalm 85:8). God speaks in the soul to the end that He may make it spiritual. And this leads us to our third point.

God Speaks by Pure Spirit

The third sign by which this purgation of sense may be recognized is that the soul can no longer meditate or reflect in the imaginative sphere of sense as it once did, no matter how it may try to do so. God now begins to communicate to the soul by pure spirit rather than through the senses as He did previously. He does this through the simple act of contemplation, to which neither the exterior nor the interior senses of the lower part of the soul can attain. From this time forward, therefore, imagination and fancy can find no support in any meditation and can gain no foothold by that means.

God Leads Them in the Way of the Spirit

With regard to this third sign, it is to be understood that the embarrassment and dissatisfaction of the faculties do not proceed from any kind of indisposition, for when this is the case, and the indisposition, which never lasts for long, comes to an end, the soul is able once again, by taking some trouble about the matter, to do what it did before, and the faculties find the support they desire.

However, in the purgation of the desire this is not so. When once the soul begins to enter therein, its inability to reflect with the faculties grows ever greater. Although it is true that at first the process is not continuous with some people, they therefore occasionally fail to abandon their pleasures and reflections of the senses. (Their weaknesses prevented them from being weaned from these immediately.) Yet this inability grows within them more and more and eventually brings the workings of sense to an end, if indeed they are to make progress, for those who walk not in the way of contemplation act very differently.

This night of dry spells is not usually continuous in their senses. At times they will have these dry spells; at other times they will not experience them. At times they cannot meditate; at other times they can. God sets them in this night only to prove them, humble them, and reform their desires, so that they will not nurture sinful gluttony in spiritual things within themselves.

His goal is to lead them in the way of the spirit, which is contemplation. However, not all who walk in the way of the spirit are brought to God by contemplation. Why this is so only God knows. This is why He never completely weans the senses of such persons from the breasts of meditations and reflections, except for only short periods and during certain seasons.

Chapter 10

THE WAYS IN WHICH SOULS ARE TO CONDUCT THEMSELVES IN THIS DARK NIGHT

The Loss of Tranquility and Peace

During the time when the soul is experiencing the dryness of the night of sense (wherein God is effecting the change of which we spoke before by drawing forth the soul from the life of sense into that of the spirit—from meditation to contemplation—wherein it no longer has any power to work or to reason with its faculties concerning the things of God), spiritual persons suffer great trials that come about not so much as a result of the dry spells, but they result from the fear they have of being lost on the road. In such a case they think that all spiritual blessing is over for them and that God has abandoned them, because they are no longer finding help or pleasure in good things.

Then they grow weary and they endeavor (as they are used to doing) to concentrate their faculties with some degree of pleasure upon some object of meditation, thinking that when they are not doing this and yet are conscious of making an effort, they are doing nothing. They make these efforts with great inner repugnance and unwillingness on the part of their souls, which had been taking delight and pleasure in being in quietness and ease instead of working with its faculties.

In so doing they have abandoned one pursuit while not drawing any profit from the other. By seeking what is prompted by their own spirits, they lose the spirit of tranquility and peace which they had before. Thus they are like those who abandon what they have done in order to do it all over again. Likewise, they are similar to those who leave a city only to reenter it, or to those who are hunting and let their prey go in order to be able to hunt it again. This of course is a useless endeavor, for the soul will gain nothing further by conducting itself in this way.

God Leads Them on a Different Road

These souls turn back at such a time if they find that there is no one who understands them. They abandon the road or they lose courage. At the least, they are hindered from going farther by the great trouble which they take in advancing along the road of meditation and reasoning. Thus they grow weary and they overwork their natures, imagining that they are failing through negligence or sin. However, this trouble that they are taking upon themselves is quite useless, for God is now leading them by a different road—that of contemplation. This road is very different from the first one they were on—the road of meditation and reasoning. The new road belongs neither to imagination nor to reasoning.

God Wants to Bring Them into His Clear and Pure Light of Love

It is well for those who find themselves in this condition to take comfort and to persevere in patience, while avoiding the afflictions cited above. Let them trust in God. He will not abandon those who seek Him with a simple and right heart. He will not fail to give them what they need for the road while He is bringing them into the clear and pure light of love. He will give them this love by means of that other dark night—the dark night of the spirit—if they merit His bringing them there.

Patient Perseverance

The way in which they are to conduct themselves in this night of sense is not to devote themselves to reasoning and meditation at all, since this is not the time for it. Instead, they should allow their souls to remain in peace and quietness, even though it may seem as if they are doing nothing and are wasting their time. It appears that way to them because of their weakness, and in that state they have no desire to think of anything.

The truth is that they will be doing sufficiently well if they have patience and persevere in prayer without making any effort. What they must do is merely to leave the soul free and unencumbered, to keep it at rest from all knowledge and thought. They must not trouble themselves about what they shall think or meditate upon, but content themselves with a peaceful and loving attentiveness toward God without anxiety, ability, and the desire to experience Him or to perceive Him. These yearnings are a disquieting influence and they distract the soul from the peaceful quiet and sweet ease of contemplation, which God grants to it at this stage.

Being at Ease and Having Freedom of Spirit

Although further ideas may come to them—that they are wasting their time and that it would be well for them to do something else, because they can neither do nor think anything in prayer—let them suffer these ideas and remain in peace, as there is nothing so important as their being at ease and having freedom of spirit. If such a soul should desire to make any effort of its own with its interior faculties, it will hinder and lose the blessings which, by means of that peace and ease of the soul, God is instilling into it and impressing upon it.

This would be like painters who are painting a face. If those they are painting moved because they desired to do something, the painters would be prevented from accomplishing anything and they would be disturbed within and distracted from what they were doing. Thus, when the soul desires to remain in inward ease and peace, any operation, affections, or attentions which appeal to it and in which it may seek to indulge, will distract, disquiet, and make it conscious of aridity and emptiness of sense. The more a soul endeavors to find support in affection and knowledge, the more it will feel the lack of these, because they can no longer be supplied to it along the road it is now on.

"Kindled in Love with Yearnings" (Stanza 1, Line 1)

It behooves such a soul to pay no heed when the operations of its faculties appear to be lost to it. Rather, the soul should desire for this to happen quickly. By not hindering the operation of infused contemplation that God is bestowing upon it, the soul can receive with more peaceful abundance and cause the spirit to be enkindled and to burn with the love which this dark and secret contemplation brings with it and sets firmly in the soul. Contemplation is a secret, peaceful, and loving infusion from God which, if it is permitted to do so, will enkindle the soul with the spirit of love—*kindled in love with yearnings.*

Chapter 11

THE EXPOUNDING OF THE FIRST THREE LINES OF THE STANZA

A Yearning toward God

This enkindling of love is usually not felt at first, because it has not begun to actually take hold upon the soul. This is due to the impurity of human nature or because the soul has not understood its own state. Therefore, it has given it no peaceful abiding place within itself. Sometimes, nevertheless, a certain yearning toward God begins to make itself felt. The more this increases, the more the soul is enkindled with love toward God without knowing or understanding how this love and affection came to it.

From time to time, though, it sees this flame and this enkindling grow so greatly within it that it desires God with the yearnings of love. This is what David referred to in the Psalms: "Thus my heart was grieved, and I was pricked in my reins. So foolish was I, and ignorant: I was as a beast before thee" (Psalm 73:21–22). David is saying that because his heart was enkindled through love of contemplation, his desires for sensual affections were changed, namely from the way of sense to the way of the spirit, which involves the aridity and cessation from all these things we are speaking of.

He goes on to say that he was dissolved into nothing and annihilated even though he did not know it was happening. This is what happens to the soul which, without knowing the way in which it goes, finds itself annihilated with respect to all things above and below that used to please it. Then it finds itself enamored with God, but does not understand what is taking place. At times the enkindling of love in the spirit grows greater and greater and the yearnings for God become so great in the soul that the person's very bones seem to be dried up by this thirst, and the natural powers seem to be fading away. Their warmth and strength seem to be perishing through the intensity of the thirst of love, and the soul feels that this thirst is a living thirst. This is what David referred to in Psalm 42:2: "My soul thirsteth for God, for the living God: when shall I come and appear before God?" His was a living thirst from his very soul. Since it is a living thirst, it actually kills. However, the vehemence of this thirst is not continuous but occasional, although as a rule the soul is accustomed to feel it to a certain degree.

Suffering That Leads to Love

It must be noted that this love is not as a rule felt at first; only the dryness and emptiness are felt at first. Then, in place of this love, which afterwards becomes gradually enkindled, what the soul experiences in the midst of these dry spells and emptiness of the faculties is habitual care and solicitude with respect to God. These are mingled with grief and fear that it is not serving Him. It is a sacrifice that is very pleasing to God, that the soul should go about afflicted and desirous for His love. This desire and care lead the soul into secret contemplation until the senses (the sensual part) have been purged of the natural affections and powers by means of the dry spells which it causes within them. Then this divine love begins to be enkindled in the spirit. Meanwhile, however, like one who has begun a cure, the soul knows only suffering in this dark and arid purgation of desire. By this means it becomes healed of many imperfections, and exercises itself in many virtues in order to make itself meet for the said love.

"Oh Happy Chance!" (Stanza 1, Line 1)

God leads the soul into this night of sense in order to purge the sense of its lower part and to subdue, unite, and bring it into conformity with the spirit by setting it in darkness and causing it to cease from meditation (mindfulness). (He does so in order to purify the spirit in order to unite it with himself.) He brings it into the night of the spirit, and (although it appears not to be so), the soul gains so many benefits that it holds it to be a "happy chance" to have escaped from the bonds and restrictions of the senses of its lower self. It does so through the dark night, and it utters this line: "Oh, happy chance!" With respect to this, it behooves us to note the benefits which the soul finds in this night. It is because of these benefits that the soul considers it a happy chance to have passed through it.

"I Went Forth without Being Observed" (Stanza 1, Line 2)

This "going forth" is understood with regard to the subjection the soul suffered in its sensual part when it sought God through operations that were so weak, so limited, and so defective. At every step it stumbled into ignorance and numerous imperfections, as we noted in our writing about the Seven Deadly Sins.

121

It is from these that the soul is freed when this dark night quenches all pleasures within it, whether they are from above or below. This makes all meditation darkness to the soul and grants it other innumerable blessings related to the acquisition of the virtues, as we shall now show. It will be a matter of great pleasure and great consolation to one who is journeying on this road to see how that which seems so severe and adverse to the soul and so contrary to spiritual pleasure works in it so many blessings. These are gained when the soul goes forth, as regards its affections and operations from all created things by means of this dark night, and when it journeys to eternal things, which involve great happiness and good fortune (the "happy chance").

This happens first because of the great blessing, which is in the quenching of the desire and affection with respect to all things. Secondly, it happens because the ones who endure and persevere in entering by the strait gate and the narrow way which lead to life are very few, as our Savior so clearly stated: "Enter ye in at the strait gate: for wide is the gate, and broad is the way, that leadeth to destruction, and many there be which go in thereat: because strait is the gate, and narrow is the way, which leadeth unto life, and few there be that find it" (Matthew 7:13–14).

The "strait gate" is the dark night of sense. The soul detaches itself from sense and strips itself of it so that it may enter this gate, and thereby it establishes itself in faith, which is a stranger to all sense. It does this so that afterwards it may journey by the narrow way, which is the other dark night—that of the spirit—and the soul enters this in order to journey to God in pure faith. It is by this means that the soul is united with God.

Because this road is so dark, narrow, and terrible, there are few that travel upon it. Nonetheless, its benefits are exceedingly great and they cannot compare with that other dark night of the senses. In the next chapter we shall look at those wonderful benefits.

Chapter 12

THE BENEFITS THAT THE DARK NIGHT OF THE SPIRIT CAUSES IN THE SOUL

Infused Contemplation

This night and purgation of the desires of the senses is a happy one for the soul, because it works in it so many blessings and benefits. (The soul, however, may feel that blessings are being taken away from it at first.) Long ago Abraham made a great feast when he weaned his son Isaac: "And the child grew, and was weaned: and Abraham made a great feast the same day that Isaac was weaned" (Genesis 21:8).

In much the same way there is great joy in Heaven when God removes the "swaddling clothes" from the soul of one of His children, sets it down from His arms, and makes it walk upon its own two feet. At this time God removes the "milk of the breast" and the soft, sweet food of children from it and causes it to eat bread with crust, and to begin to enjoy the food of more mature, robust persons. This food, in the midst of the aridities and darkness of the senses, is now given to the spirit, which is dry and emptied of all the sweetness of the senses. The food of which I speak is the infused contemplation that God imparts to the soul.

The Knowledge of Oneself and One's Misery

The first and principal benefit that is caused by the arid and dark night of contemplation is the knowledge of oneself and of one's misery. All the favors God grants to the soul are wrapped in this knowledge. The dryness and the emptiness of the faculties, which the soul experienced previously and

123

the difficulty which it finds in good works, make it recognize its own lowliness and misery, which during the time of its prosperity it was unable to see.

There is an excellent illustration of this in the Book of Exodus, where God, wishing to humble the children of Israel and desiring that they should truly know themselves, commanded them to take away and strip off the festal garments and adornments they were wearing in the wilderness. God said to Moses, "Say unto the children of Israel, Ye are a stiffnecked people: I will come up into the midst of thee in a moment, and consume thee: therefore now put off thy ornaments from thee, that I may know what to do unto thee. And the children of Israel stripped themselves of their ornaments by the mount Horeb" (Exodus 33:5 6).

God wanted them to remove the festal ornaments and put on everyday working clothes, which they did. It was as if He was saying, "Inasmuch as the attire that you wear, which is proper to festivals and rejoicing, causes you to feel less humble concerning yourselves than you should, take those things off so that you will see yourselves clothed with vileness and know that you have no merit. In this way you will know who you truly are."

When this happens, the soul realizes the truth that it never knew before, the truth of its own misery. At the time when it was clad for a festival and found in God and had much pleasure, consolation and support, it was somewhat more satisfied and contented, since it thought it was serving God to some extent. It is true that such souls may not have this idea explicitly in their minds, but some suggestion of it at least is implanted in them by the satisfaction which they find in their pleasant experiences.

Now that the soul has put on its other working attire—that of dryness and abandonment—and now that its first lights have turned to darkness, it possesses these lights more truly in this virtue of self-knowledge, which is so excellent and so necessary, considering itself now as nothing and experiencing no satisfaction in itself, for it sees that it does nothing of itself and cannot do anything.

The smallness of this self-satisfaction, together with the soul's affliction over not serving God, is considered and esteemed by God as being greater than all the consolations which the soul formerly experienced and the works which it wrought, no matter how great they were. It's important to realize that they were the occasion of much ignorance and many imperfections. And from this attire of aridity proceeds, as from their fount and source of knowledge, not only the things which we have already described, but also the benefits which we shall now describe, and many more which will regrettably have to be omitted.

Communing With God

In the first place, the soul learns to commune with God with more respect and more courtesy, such as a soul must ever observe in its communion with the Most High. The soul did not know this during its prosperous times of comfort and consolation, for that comforting favor it experienced made its craving for God somewhat bolder than was fitting and even discourteous and ill-considered.

This is what happened to Moses when he perceived that God was speaking to him; he was blinded by pleasure and desire and, without any further consideration, he would have made bold to go to Him if God had not commanded him to stay and take off his shoes. Through this incident we are shown the respect and discretion that come from the detachment of desire, wherewith a man or woman is able to truly commune with God. When Moses obeyed, he became so discreet and so attentive that the Scripture says that not only did he not make a bold move to draw near to God, but he dared not even look at Him. He took off the shoes of his desires and pleasures and became very conscious of his wretchedness in the sight of God. This befits one who is about to hear the voice of God.

Similarly, God granted a time of preparation to Job in order that he might be able to speak with Him. This did not consist in the delights and glories Job said that he desired to have in God, but in leaving him naked upon a dung heap: "So went Satan forth from the presence of the LORD, and smote Job with sore boils from the sole of his foot unto his crown. And he took him a potsherd to scrape himself withal; and he sat down among the ashes" (Job 2:7–8).

Job had been abandoned and persecuted by his friends, and he was filled with anguish, bitterness, and pain. He was sitting on a dung heap that was crawling with worms. It was then that the Most High God lifted him up from the dunghill and was pleased to come down and speak with Job face to face, revealing to him the depths and heights of His great wisdom in a way that Job had never known or experienced during the time of his prosperity.

Light Shining in the Darkness

Another excellent benefit that is found in this dark night and the aridity of the desires that come from the senses, is that the dark night of the desire vanishes in the light. The prophet said, "And if thou draw out thy soul to the hungry, and satisfy the afflicted soul; then shall thy light rise in obscurity, and thy darkness be as the noon day" (Isaiah 58:10). God will enlighten the soul and give it knowledge, not only of its lowliness and wretchedness, as we have said, but likewise of the greatness and excellence of God.

As well as quenching the desires and pleasures and attachments of the senses, God cleanses and frees the understanding, that it may understand the truth. Pleasure of sense and desire, even though the desire may be for spiritual things, darkens and obstructs the spirit. Furthermore, that aridity of sense enlightens and quickens the understanding,

126

as Isaiah says: "From the time that it goeth forth it shall take you: for morning by morning shall it pass over, by day and by night: and it shall be a vexation only to understand the report" (Isaiah 28:19). Vexation causes us to understand how the soul that is empty and unencumbered, as is necessary for God's influence to take effect, is instructed supernaturally by God in His divine wisdom, through this dark and arid night of contemplation. This instruction was not imparted to the soul when it was enjoying those first joys and sweetness.

As We Know Ourselves, We Begin to Know God

Isaiah gives us a clear explanation of what we have just discussed: "Whom shall he teach knowledge? and whom shall he make to understand doctrine? them that are weaned from the milk, and drawn from the breasts" (Isaiah 28:9). Here we see that the first milk of spiritual sweetness is no preparation for divine influence in our lives. We also see that there is no preparation in attachment that is provided by the breasts of delectable meditations that belong to the faculties of the senses, which give the soul pleasure. Such preparation consists rather in the lack of the one and withdrawal from the other.

In order to listen to God, the soul needs to stand upright and to be detached from the affections and the senses. This is what the prophet Habakkuk said about himself: "I will stand upon my watch, and set me upon the tower, and will watch to see what he will say unto me, and what I shall answer when I am reproved" (Habakkuk 2:1). When Habakkuk said he would stand upon his watch, he was referring to the detachment of desire. When he said that he would make his step firm, he was saying that he would not meditate through the senses in order to be able to contemplate—to understand that which would come to him from God.

Through these insights and examples we see that self-knowledge comes from this arid night. Knowledge of God, like a fountain, comes from another foundation, which caused Saint Augustine to say to God, "Let me know myself, Lord, and I shall know Thee." For, as the philosophers say, one extreme can be well-known by another.

Knowledge of the Glory of God

In order to prove more completely how efficacious this night of sense is—with all its dryness and desolation—in bringing light to the soul from God, let's look at what David had to say: "O GOD, thou art my God; early will I seek thee: my soul thirsteth for thee, my flesh longeth for thee in a dry and thirsty land, where no water is; to see thy power and thy glory, so as I have seen thee in the sanctuary" (Psalm 63:1–2). It is a wondrous thing that David should say that the means and the preparation for his knowledge of the glory of God were not the spiritual delights and the many pleasures which he had experienced, but they were the aridities and detachments of his sensual nature, which is here to be understood by his phrase, "a dry and thirsty land." It is no less wondrous that he should describe, as the road to his perception and vision of the virtue of God, not the divine meditations and conceptions of which he had often made use, but his being unable to form any conception of God and of oneself in this dark night with all its aridities and voids. This does not lead to a knowledge of Him that is of the same plenitude and abundance that comes from the dark night of the spirit, since this is only, as it were, the beginning of that other night.

Spiritual Humility

Likewise, from the aridities and voids of the night of desire, the soul draws spiritual humility, which is the contrary virtue to the first Deadly Sin which, as we said, is spiritual pride. Through this humility, which is acquired by the knowledge of one's self, the soul is purged from all those imperfections into which it fell with respect to the sin of pride during the times of prosperity. It sees itself as being so dry and miserable that the idea never even occurs to it that it is making better progress than others or outstripping them, as it believed itself to be doing before. On the contrary, it recognizes that others are making better progress than itself.

The Love of Neighbors

Hence arises the love of neighbors, for the soul esteems them and judges them not as it used to do, when it saw that it had great fervor itself while others did not. It is aware of its own wretchedness, which it keeps before its eyes to such an extent that it never forgets it and never takes occasion to set its eyes on anyone else. David described this most wonderfully (when he was in this night): "I was dumb with silence, I held my peace, even from good; and my sorrow was stirred" (Psalm 39:2). Thus, he says that because it seemed to him that the good that was in his soul had so completely departed that not only did he neither speak nor find any language concerning it but, with respect to the good of others, he was likewise mute because of his grief over the knowledge of his own misery.

The Sweeping Away of All Imperfections

In this condition souls become submissive and obedient upon the spiritual road. This is because when they see their own misery, not only do they hear what is being taught to them, but they even desire that anyone would set them on the way and tell them what they ought to do. The old affective presumption that they sometimes had in their prosperity has been taken from them. Finally all other imperfections, which we noted with respect to spiritual pride, are swept away from them.

Chapter 13

OTHER BENEFITS THAT THIS DARK NIGHT OF SENSES CAUSES IN THE SOUL

Humility and Readiness

With respect to the soul's imperfections regarding spiritual avarice, because of which it coveted various spiritual things but found no satisfaction in them due to its covetousness for the desire and pleasure which it found therein, this arid and dark night has now greatly reformed it. Now it does not find the pleasure and sweetness which it once looked for, but rather it finds affliction and lack of sweetness. It now has such moderate recourse to them that it might possibly now lose through defective use what it has previously lost through excess.

As a rule, God gives humility and readiness to those He leads into this night, along with a lack of sweetness, so that they may do what is commanded for God's sake alone. Thus they no longer seek profit in many things, because they no longer find any pleasure in them.

Freed From Impurities

With respect to spiritual luxury, it is likewise clearly seen that through the dryness and lack of sensory sweetness, which the soul now finds in spiritual things, it is freed from those impurities which we have noted, impurities that proceeded from the pleasure which overflowed from the spirit into the realm of the senses.

The Curbing of Desire

With regard to the imperfections from which the soul frees itself in this dark night with regard to the fourth sin, which is spiritual gluttony, they may be referred to above, but

130

not entirely, for those imperfections are truly innumerable. Thus, I shall not detail them here, for we have to go on to other subjects which are graver still. Let it suffice for us to say that the understanding of the innumerable benefits which, over and above those already mentioned, the soul gains in this night with respect to the sin of spiritual gluttony, to say that it frees itself from all those imperfections which have been described and from many other and greater evils and vile abominations, which have not been discussed, but into which many have fallen, because they did not reform their desire concerning the inordinate love of spiritual sweetness.

In this arid and dark night into which God has set the soul, He has restrained its concupiscence (sexual desires) and curbed its desires so that the soul cannot feed upon any pleasure or sweetness of sense, whether from above or from below. He continues to do this in such a manner that the soul is subjected, reformed, and repressed with respect to all strong desires. It loses the strength of its passions and desires, and it becomes sterile, because it no longer consults its likings. This is similar to the situation that takes place when one is accustomed to take milk from the breast and the milk dries up. The desires of the soul are dried up as well.

Besides these things, other admirable benefits are derived from this spiritual sobriety, for when the soul's strong desires are quenched, it is able to live in spiritual tranquility and peace. When strong desires no longer reign within the soul, there is no longer any disturbance, and peace and God's consolation take over.

Remembrance of God

A second benefit comes to the soul as well. It now habitually remembers God with fear and a dread of backsliding along the spiritual road. This is a truly great benefit that arises from the aridity and purgation of desire. The soul is purified and cleansed of the imperfections that had been clinging to it because of strong desires and affections, which always result in the deadening and darkening of the soul.

Patience and Other Virtues

There is another very great benefit for the soul in this dark night, and that is that it begins to practice several virtues at once. An example would be patience and longsuffering, which are often called upon in these times of emptiness and aridity, when the soul must endure and persevere in its spiritual exercises without consolation and pleasure.

It now learns to practice the love of God since it is no longer moved by the pleasures of attraction and sweetness. The soul is now moved exclusively by God. It likewise practices the virtue of fortitude, because during the times of difficulty through which it passes, strength comes from weakness. The soul becomes strong. In short, all the virtues (theological, cardinal, and moral, both in body and spirit) are now practiced by the soul during these times of darkness and dryness.

David's Experience

We have just described four benefits that the soul obtains during this dark night: delight of peace, habitual remembrance and thought of God, cleanness and purity of soul, and the practice of all the virtues. David describes what this wonderful experience is like: "I remembered God, and was troubled: I complained, and my spirit was overwhelmed. Selah. Thou holdest mine eyes waking: I am so troubled that I cannot speak" (Psalm 77:3–4). And then he says: "I call to remembrance my song in the night: I commune with mine own heart: and my spirit made diligent search" (Psalm 77:6). Here, David is describing how he swept his heart clean from all affections.

Meekness

We have covered four of the spiritual sins. Now let us take a look at the other three—wrath, envy, and sloth. The soul is purged from these as well through the drying up of desire. In so doing, it has acquired the opposite virtues, because it has been softened and humbled by the hardships, temptations, and trials it has endured. God allowed the soul to face these so it would learn to experience meekness before Him, other people, and itself. Therefore, the soul is no longer disturbed and angry with itself because of its own faults, neither is it angry with its neighbors. Nor is it displeased with God, and it no longer complains to Him for not bringing holiness to it.

A Virtuous Envy

As regards envy, the soul now has charity toward others. If it has any envy at all, it is not a sinful kind of envy; rather, it is a virtuous envy in that it desires to imitate others. This is a great virtue, and it is far different from the kind of envy the soul had before, when it was grieved because others were preferred before it and were seemingly given greater advantage.

A New Kind of Weariness

The vicious kind of sloth and irksomeness which the soul used to experience has gone as well. In the past, those sins proceeded from the spiritual pleasures which the soul sometimes experienced and sought after when it could not find them. The soul's new weariness does not proceed from the insufficiency of pleasure, because God has taken from it pleasure in all things, as He has purged the soul of its desires.

The Purest Spiritual Sweetness and Love

Besides the benefits we've just mentioned, the soul attains innumerable others as well, by means of the arid

133

contemplation we discussed before. Often, in the midst of these times of dryness and hardship, God communicates to the soul when it least expects it. He communicates the purest spiritual sweetness and love, along with a spiritual knowledge that is sometimes very delicate, and each manifestation of it grows in its benefits to the soul. At first, the soul might not think this is so, for the spiritual influence it gains is very delicate and cannot be perceived by the senses.

The Fruit of the Holy Spirit and Spiritual Deliverance

Now that the soul is purged from the affections and desires aroused by the senses, it has obtained spiritual liberty, and it gains the fruit of the Holy Spirit. It is also wondrously delivered from the hands of its three enemies—the devil, the world, and the flesh. Now that its pleasure and delight from the sensory realm have been completely quenched, neither the devil nor the world nor any kinds of sensuality have any strength whereby they are able to make war against the spirit.

A Desire to Please God

The times of dryness have caused the soul to journey in all purity into the love of God, because it is no longer influenced by the pleasure and sweetness of actions and desires as it used to be. Now its all-consuming desire is to please God. As a result, it is neither presumptuous nor self-satisfied, as it once was. Now it is timid and fearful with regard to itself, because it finds in itself no satisfaction whatsoever. This is what causes it to have a holy fear, which preserves the virtues and causes them to increase. The times of dryness quenched all natural energy and strong desire, except for the wonderful pleasure God infuses into it.

Concern for God and Yearnings to Serve Him

Souls who experience the arid night begin to grow in their concern for God and their yearnings to serve Him. The

134

breasts of sensuality that had once nourished the soul have now dried up and there remains nothing in that aridity and detachment except for the yearning to serve God, which is a very pleasing thing to Him. David said, "The sacrifices of God are a broken spirit: a broken and a contrite heart, O God, thou wilt not despise" (Psalm 51:17). As David points out, an afflicted spirit is a sacrifice to God.

"I Went Forth Without Being Observed" (Stanza 1, Line 2)

When the soul knows that in the arid purgation through which it has passed, it has derived and attained so many precious benefits as those which we are describing, it begins to cry, "*Oh, happy chance!—I went forth without being observed.*" (Stanza 1, Lines 1 and 2 from "Stanzas of the Soul.")

Yes, the soul went forth from the bonds and subjection of the desires of the senses and affections "without being observed." This means that the three enemies of the soul (the world, the flesh, and the devil) are no longer able to hold it back; whereas before, they had bound the soul in its desires and pleasures and prevented it from going forth for itself to the liberty of the love of God. Those enemies can no longer do battle with the soul.

Calmness

The four passions of the soul—joy, grief, hope, and fear—are calmed through continual mortification. The natural desires have been lulled to sleep in the sensual nature of the soul through habitual times of aridity. The harmony of the senses and the interior faculties have caused a suspension of labor and a cessation from the work of meditation within the lower part of the soul. No enemy can obstruct spiritual liberty any longer, and the house is at rest and quiet.

135

Chapter 14

THE EXPOUNDING OF THE
LAST VERSE OF THE FIRST STANZA

"My House Now Being at Rest" (Stanza 1, last verse)

When the house of the senses and sensuality is at rest because it was mortified, its passions were quenched, and its desires were put to sleep, as a result of the blessed night of the purgation of the senses, the soul went forth. It set out upon the road and way of the spirit, which is that of progress and proficiency. It is called the way of illumination or of infused contemplation. This is where God himself feeds and refreshes the soul without meditation or any help whatsoever from the soul.

Such is the night and the purgation of the senses in the soul. Those who must eventually enter the other and more formidable night of the spirit in order to pass into the divine union of the love of God (for not all, but just a very few ever get there), must go through additional trials and tribulations, which will last a very long time, longer in some than in others. These are further trials and temptations related to the senses. To some even Satan will present himself by way of the spirit of fornication, so that he may buffet their senses with abominable and violent temptations and trouble their spirits with vile considerations and representations, which are most visible to the imagination. At times these things represent a greater affliction than that of death itself.

Blasphemy

At other times in the night, the spirit of blasphemy is added to the other temptations and trials. This spirit roams abroad, setting intolerable blasphemies in the paths of all the conceptions and thoughts of the soul. It sometimes suggests these blasphemies to the soul with such violence that the soul almost utters them, which presents it with a grave torment.

A Perverse Spirit

At other times a particularly abominable spirit, which Isaiah calls "a perverse spirit"—*spiritus vertiginis*—is allowed to molest them. The prophet writes, "The LORD hath mingled a perverse spirit in the midst thereof: and they have caused Egypt to err in every work thereof, as a drunken man staggereth in his vomit" (Isaiah 19:14). This spirit will molest them not in order that they may fall, but that it may try them. This spirit darkens their senses in such a way that it fills them with numerous scruples and perplexities that are so confusing that, as they attempt to judge, they can never by any means be satisfied concerning them, neither can they find any help for their judgment in counsel or thought. This is one of the severest goads and horrors of this night, and it is very closely akin to that which passes in the night of the spirit.

Leading to the Other Night

These are the storms and trials which God sends to the soul in this night, and the purgation of the senses He provides for those He purposes to lead into the other night (though not all reach it). The goal is that when they have been chastened and buffeted, they may in this way continually exercise and prepare themselves and continually accustom their senses and faculties to the union of wisdom, which is to be bestowed upon them in that other night.

If the soul is not exercised and proved with trials and temptations, it cannot quicken its sense of wisdom. Jeremiah bears witness to this truth:

> "I have surely heard Ephraim bemoaning himself
> thus; Thou hast chastised me, and I was chastised,

as a bullock unaccustomed to the yoke; turn thou me, and I shall be turned; for thou art the LORD my God" (Jeremiah 31:18).

The most proper form of this chastisement for one who will enter into wisdom is that of the interior trials which we are here describing. It is these kinds of trials that most effectively purge the senses of all favors and consolations to which they were affected with natural weakness, and by which the soul is truly humiliated in preparation for the exaltation which it is to experience.

How God Purges Us

We don't know how long each soul will be held in this fasting and penance of the senses. Nothing can be said with any certainty about this at all, for all do not experience it in the same way, and not all encounter the same temptations. This is meted out by the will of God in conformity with the greater or smaller degree of imperfections which each soul has to purge away. In conformity, likewise, with the degree of love of union to which God is pleased to raise it, He will humble it with greater or less intensity or in greater or less time.

Those who have the disposition and greater strength to suffer will be purged with greater intensity and more quickly. But those who are very weak are kept for a long time in this night, and these God purges very gently and with slight temptations. Habitually, too, He gives them refreshments of sense so that they may not fall away, and only after a long time do they attain to purity of perfection in this life; some, however, never attain to it at all. The latter are neither properly in the night nor properly out of it. Although they make little progress, they continue in it in order to gain humility and self-knowledge.

God exercises them for certain periods and at certain times (or for certain days) in those temptations and dryness. In other times and seasons He assists them with consolations, lest they should grow faint and return to seek the consolations of the world. Other souls which are much weaker God will accompany himself. At one time He will appear to them and then move farther away. This is so He may exercise them in His love, for without such turnings away, they would never learn to reach God.

The Union of Love

Those souls who are to pass on to that happy and high estate—the union of love—will desire, as a rule, to remain for a long time in the dryness and temptations, no matter how quickly God may lead them. This has been experienced by souls time and again. Now it is time for us to begin to discuss the second night.

BOOK II

THE DARK NIGHT
OF THE SPIRIT

Chapter 1

THE BEGINNING OF
THE DARK NIGHT OF THE SPIRIT

How to Enter into the Dark Night of the Spirit

The soul which God is about to advance onward is not led by Him into this night of the spirit as soon as it emerges from the dryness and trials of the first purgation and the night of the senses. Rather, it is likely to desire to wait a long time, perhaps even years, after leaving the state of beginners. It is as if the soul is coming from a narrow prison or a rigorous time of incarceration. This newfound freedom enables it to go about the things of God with greater freedom, satisfaction of the soul, and abundant and inward delight that it did at the beginning before it entered the said night.

Its imagination and faculties are no longer bound as they were before by meditation and anxiety of spirit, since now it very readily finds in its spirit the most serene and loving contemplation and spiritual sweetness without the labor that meditation had required. The purgation of the soul is not complete (for the principal part of it—the spirit—remains wanting). The purgation of sense, however violent it may have been, is not yet complete and perfect. This means that there are certain necessities, such as dryness, darkness, and perils, which are sometimes more intense than those that were experienced in the past, that will serve as tokens and heralds of the coming night of the spirit, and they are not as long in duration as the night which is to come.

Having passed through a period or many periods involving this night and tempest, the soul soon returns to its desired serenity. After this manner God purges certain souls which are not to rise to so high a degree of love as are others. He brings them at times, sometimes for short periods, into this night of contemplation and purgation of the spirit, causing night to come upon them, followed by the dawn; and He does this frequently, so that the words of David may be fulfilled: "He casteth forth his ice like morsels: who can stand before his cold?" (Psalm 147:17). David is telling us that God sends forth His icy crystals—His contemplation—like morsels, although these morsels of dark contemplation are never as intense as that which is experienced during the terrible night of contemplation, which we will describe. It is this terrible night of contemplation that God brings to the soul so that He may lead it on into complete union with Him.

The Pleasures of the Spirit

This sweetness, then, and this interior pleasure which we are describing and which progressive souls find and experience in their spirits so easily and so abundantly, is communicated to them in much greater abundance than ever before. It overflows into their senses more than ever, more than before the purgation of their senses. Inasmuch as their senses are now purer, they can more easily feel the pleasures of the spirit after its manner. However, as this sensual part of the soul is weak and incapable of experiencing the strong things of the spirit, it follows that these people, by reason of this spiritual communication which is made to their sensual parts, will endure therein many frailties and sufferings and weaknesses of the stomach. In consequence of this they will grow fatigued in spirit.

144

Hence, the communications that are granted to these souls cannot be very strong or very intense or very spiritual, as is required for divine union with God. This is because of the weakness and corruption of the sensual nature which still has a part in them. Hence arise the raptures and trances and dislocations of the bones, which always happen when the communications are not purely spiritual; that is, they are not given to the spirit alone, as are those of the perfect who are purified by the second night of the spirit and in whom these raptures and torments of the body no longer exist, since they are enjoying liberty of spirit and their senses are now neither clouded nor transported.

Imperfections and Perils

For those who are more advanced to enter this night of the spirit, in must be understood that certain imperfections and perils belong to them.

Chapter 2

THE IMPERFECTIONS EXPERIENCED BY THOSE WHO ARE MORE ADVANCED

Two Kinds of Imperfections

Those who are more advanced have two kinds of imperfections. One is habitual; the other is actual. The habitual imperfections are the imperfect habits and affections which have remained in the spirit all the time. These are like roots which the purgation of the senses has been unable to penetrate. The difference between the purgation of these imperfections and the purgation of the others is like the difference between a root and a branch. It is also comparable to the difference between removing a stain that is fresh and one that is longstanding.

The purgation of the senses is only the entrance and beginning of the contemplation that leads to the purgation of the spirit. This serves to accommodate sense to spirit rather than uniting spirit with God. The stains of "the old man" remain in the spirit even though the spirit thinks this is not so, because it cannot perceive them. If these stains are not removed with the soap and strong lye that comes from the purgation of this dark night, the spirit will be unable to come to the purity that is needed for union with God.

Habitual Imperfections

These souls have the *hebetudo mentis* (the deadening of the mind) and the natural roughness which everyone acquires through sin. The spirit must be enlightened, refined, and focused by the afflictions and perils of that dark night. These habitual imperfections belong to all those who have not passed beyond this state of the more advanced. They cannot coexist with the perfect state of union through love.

Actual Imperfections

The actual imperfections are quite different from the habitual ones. Some, whose spiritual good is so superficial and so readily affected by the senses, fall into greater difficulties and dangers—the ones we described at the beginning of this treatise. They find so many and such abundant spiritual communications and apprehensions, both in sense and in spirit, that they oftentimes see imaginary and spiritual visions, which may be demonic deceptions. The devil takes delight in impressing these apprehensions and feelings upon the soul, and he deludes it with great ease unless the soul takes the precaution of resigning itself to God and of protecting itself from these visions and feelings by means of faith.

146

In this state the devil will cause many to believe in vain visions and false prophecies, and he strives to make the soul presume that God and the saints are speaking with them. In this way they begin to trust their own fancy. The devil will also fill them with presumption and pride, so much so that they become attracted by vanities and arrogance. This leads them to engage in certain outward acts that appear to be holy but are not, such as raptures and other fleshly and soulish manifestations.

Thus, they become bold with God, and they lose holy fear, which is the key and the custodian of all the virtues. In some of these souls many falsehoods and deceits begin to multiply, and this causes it to seem highly unlikely that they will ever return to the pure road of virtue and true spirituality. They fall into these miseries because they are beginning to give themselves over to spiritual feelings and apprehensions with a false sense of security, even though at one time they were beginning to make some real progress along the way.

Purification Is Necessary

There is much more that I could say regarding these imperfections and how they become incurable because these souls consider themselves to be more spiritual than they really are—more spiritual even than others. I shall only add one thing at this stage, in order to prove how necessary it is for these souls to go further into the dark night of the spirit so that they can experience complete purgation. No matter how strenuously they may have labored, they will never be free from these many natural affections and imperfect habits until they experience spiritual purification, which is absolutely necessary if a soul is to enter into union with God.

The Second Night of the Spirit

Inasmuch as the lower part of the soul still has a share in the spiritual communications we have mentioned, they

147

cannot be as intense, as pure, and as strong as necessary to enter into union with God. Therefore, in order to gain this union, the soul must enter into the second night of the spirit in which it must strip sense and spirit perfectly from all these apprehensions and from all sweetness. Then it must be made to walk in dark and pure faith, which is the proper and adequate means whereby the soul is united with God.

Chapter 3

ANNOTATIONS FOR THAT WHICH FOLLOWS

The Purging of the Spiritual and the Sensual

These more advanced souls have spent a great deal of time in feeding their senses with sweet communications. As a result, their sensual part has become attracted to and delighted by spiritual pleasure, which came to it from the spirit. Now it may be united with the spirit and made one with it by each part after its own manner, eating of one and the same spiritual food from one and the same dish. They do so as one person now, a person who has a sole intent—that they may be united and brought into agreement and, thus united, may be prepared for the endurance of the stern and severe purgation of the spirit which awaits them.

In this purgation, these two parts of the soul—the spiritual and the sensual—must be completely purged, since the one is never truly purged without the other. The purgation of sense becomes effective when that of the spirit has begun. The dark night of the senses may and should be called a kind of correction and restraint of the desire rather than actual purgation. The reason is that all the imperfections and disorders of the sensual part have their strength and root in the spirit, where all habits, both good and bad, are brought

148

into subjection. Thus, until these are purged, the rebellions and depravities of the senses cannot be purged thoroughly.

Great Fortitude is Needed

During this second dark night of the spirit, both parts of the soul are purged together, and it is for this end that it was good that it passed through the corrections of the first night and the period of tranquility that proceeded from it. This enables the senses to be united with the spirit, and both are purged after a certain manner. They may then be able to suffer with a greater degree of fortitude.

Very great fortitude is needed during such a violent and severe purgation, because if the weakness of the lower part has not first been corrected and fortitude has not been acquired from God through the sweet and delectable communion which the soul has afterwards enjoyed with Him, its nature will not have the strength or the disposition to bear it.

Divine Stripping of the Faculties, Affections, and Feelings

These more advanced souls still have a long way to go, because they are at a very low stage of progress. They still follow their own natures closely in the intercourse and dealings they have with God. The gold of their spirits has not yet been purified and refined, and they still think of God, speak of God, experience God, and feel God as a little child does. Paul speaks about this in his first letter to the Corinthians: "When I was a child, I spake as a child, I understood as a child, I thought as a child: but when I became a man, I put away childish things" (1 Corinthians 13:11).

They have not yet reached perfection, which is the union of the soul with God. When they reach that union, they will be able to work great things in the spirit, even as fully grown individuals, and their works and faculties will then be divine rather than human. With this end in mind, therefore, God is pleased to strip them of "the old man" and clothe them with "the new man," who is created according to God, as Paul has directed: "And that ye put on the new man, which after God is created in righteousness and true holiness" (Ephesians 4:24).

The transformation described by Paul refers to newness in everything, including the senses. Therefore, God strips away their faculties, affections, and feelings, both spiritual and sensual, both outward and inward. As a result, the understanding becomes dark, the will becomes dry, the memory is empty, and the affections experience the deepest afflictions of bitterness and constraint. This takes away the pleasure and experience of spiritual blessings which the soul had enjoyed previously.

This is a principle of the spiritual life, and it opens the way for the spirit to be united with the Spirit, which is the union of love. The Lord works all this in the soul by way of a pure and dark contemplation, as is explained in the first stanza of my opening poem. Although we originally interpreted this stanza with reference to the first night of the senses, it is principally understood by the soul during this second night of the spirit, because it relates to the purification of the soul.

Chapter 4

THE EXPOSITION OF THE FIRST STANZA

On a dark night, kindled in love with yearnings—
Oh, happy chance!
I went forth without being observed,
My house being now at rest.

"Stanzas of the Soul"— First Stanza

Going Forth

Let's begin by interpreting this first stanza with reference to purgation, contemplation, or detachment (poverty) of spirit, which are almost all the same in this context. The soul speaks thusly: In poverty and without protection or support in all the apprehensions of my soul—that is, in the darkness of my understanding and the constraint of my will, in affliction and anguish with respect to memory—and remaining in the dark in pure faith, which is a dark night for the natural faculties, the will alone is being touched by grief and afflictions and yearnings for the love of God. In this state I went forth from myself—from my low manner of understanding, from my weak mode of loving, and from my poor and limited manner of experiencing God without being hindered by sensuality or the devil.

A Great Happiness and a Good Chance

This was a great happiness and a good chance for me; for when the faculties and the passions, desires, and affections of my soul had been perfectly annihilated and calmed (with these I had experienced God only in a lowly manner), I went forth from my own human dealings and operations to the operations and dealings of God. In other words, my understanding went forth from itself by turning from the human and natural to the divine. When it is united with God by this purgation, its understanding no longer comes through its natural light and vigor, but through the divine wisdom with which it has become united.

My will went forth from itself, becoming divine. Being united with divine love, it no longer loves with its natural strength in a lowly manner but with strength and purity from the Holy Spirit. Thus the will, which is now near to God, no longer acts in a human manner. Similarly, the memory has been transformed into eternal apprehensions of glory. Finally, by means of this dark night and purgation of the old man, all the energies and affections of the soul are wholly renewed into a divine temper and delight.

There follows this line: *"On a dark night."*

Chapter 5

THE FIRST LINE OF THE POEM:
HOW THIS DARK CONTEMPLATION IS NOT
ONLY NIGHT FOR THE SOUL, BUT IS ALSO
GRIEF AND PURGATION

An Inflowing of God Into the Soul

This dark night is an inflowing of God into the soul, which purges it from its ignorance and habitual, natural, and spiritual imperfections. This is known by contemplatives as "infused contemplation" or mystical theology. God secretly teaches the soul and instructs it in the perfection of love without it having to do much of anything, or even understanding what the manner of infused contemplation actually is. It is the loving wisdom of God, and He produces striking effects in the soul by purging and illuminating it. He prepares it for the union of love with God. The same loving wisdom that purges the blessed spirits and enlightens them is that which here purges the soul and illuminates it.

Divine Light and Wisdom

Why is the divine light, which illuminates and purges the soul from its ignorance, called here by the soul "a dark night"? There are two reasons why this divine wisdom is not only night and darkness for the soul, but is also affliction and torment. The first is because of the height of divine wisdom, which transcends the talent of the soul, and therefore is darkness to it. The second is the vileness and impurity of the soul, which causes a painful affliction, and it is very dark indeed.

A Ray of Darkness

In order to prove the first point, we must here assume a certain doctrine of philosophy, which says that the clearer and more manifest divine things are in themselves, the darker and more hidden they are to the soul. Similarly, the clearer the light is, the more it blinds and darkens the pupils of the owl; and the more we look at the sun, the greater is the darkness it causes in our vision by overcoming and overwhelming it through its own weaknesses.

In the same way, when the divine light of contemplation assails the soul that is not yet wholly enlightened, it causes spiritual darkness within it. Not only does it overcome it, but it likewise overwhelms it and darkens the act of its natural intelligence. For this reason Saint Dionysius and other mystical theologians call this infused contemplation a "ray of darkness." This is to say that for the soul that is not enlightened and purged, the natural strength of the intellect is transcended and overwhelmed by its great supernatural light. David wrote, "For the LORD most high is terrible; he is a great King over all the earth" (Psalm 47:2). In saying this,

David is suggesting that near to God and around Him are darkness and clouds. He is not saying, however, that this is a fact, but that it seems so to our weak understanding, which has been blinded and darkened by so vast a light—a light to which it cannot attain.

David also said, "At the brightness that was before him his thick clouds passed, hail stones and coals of fire" (Psalm 18:12). Here David is saying that clouds passed through the great splendor of God's presence. This refers to the clouds that are between God and our understanding. It is for this cause that when God sends the illuminating ray of His secret wisdom to the soul that is not yet transformed, thick darkness in the understanding results.

An Inner Struggle

It is clear that this dark contemplation in its beginnings is painful to the soul. The divinely infused contemplation has many excellences that are extremely good, but the soul that receives them without being purged has many miseries that are extremely bad. Hence it follows that as two contrary things cannot coexist in one subject, namely the soul; it must of necessity go through additional pain and suffering. This happens because the soul is the subject wherein these two contrary forces war against each other, working one against the other continually. This happens as a result of the purgation of the imperfections of the soul through contemplation. By inductive reasoning we shall now try to prove this.

Great Grief and Pain

Because the light and wisdom of this contemplation is most bright and pure, and the soul which it assails is dark and impure, it follows that the soul suffers great pain which it receives within itself. This is similar to what happens when eyes that have been dimmed by visual problems and are impure and weak are assaulted by a bright light. It

154

causes great pain to those eyes. When the soul suffers the direct assault of divine light, its pain, which results from its impurity, is immense. When this pure light assails the soul in order to expel its impurities, the soul feels itself to be so impure and miserable that it believes that God has gone against it and even thinks that it has set itself up against God. This causes it great grief and pain, because it now believes that God has cast it away. This is one of the greatest trials Job had to go through. He said, "I have sinned; what shall I do unto thee, O thou preserver of men? why hast thou set me as a mark against thee, so that I am a burden to myself?" (Job 7:20).

By means of the pure light (the same light Job had received), the soul now sees its impurity clearly, yet somewhat darkly. It knows clearly that it is unworthy of God, or of any creature for that matter. What gives it the most pain, however, is that it thinks it will never be worthy and that all good things are over for it. This is caused by the profound immersion of its spirit in the knowledge and realization of its evils and miseries. The divine and dark light now reveals all these things to the eye, that it may see clearly how in its own strength it can never have anything else. This helps us to understand what David meant when he wrote, "When thou with rebukes dost correct man for iniquity, thou makest his beauty to consume away like a moth: surely every man is vanity" (Psalm 39:11).

Pain from Weakness

The second way in which the soul suffers pain is because of its weakness—natural, moral, and spiritual weakness. When divine contemplation assails the soul with a certain force in order to strengthen and subdue it, it suffers such pain in its weakness that it nearly faints from it. This is especially so at certain times when it is assailed with somewhat greater force; for sense and spirit, as if beneath some immense and dark load, are in such great pain and agony that the soul would find advantage and relief in death. This was what Job was experiencing when he said, "Will he plead against me with his great power? No; but he would put strength in me" (Job 23:6).

God's Light and Gentle Hand Seem Heavy to the Soul

Beneath the power of this oppression and weight, the soul feels itself so far from being favored that it actually thinks, and correctly so, that all sources of help have vanished for it, and there is no one who will take pity upon it. Job experienced this as well: "Have pity upon me, have pity upon me, O ye my friends; for the hand of God hath touched me" (Job 19:21).

The soul's weakness and impurity should now be so great that, though the hand of God is so light and gentle, the soul now feels that it is very heavy and even contrary, though it neither weighs it down nor rests upon it. It only touches it in a very merciful way. God does this in order to grant favors to the soul, not to chastise it. (See Job 7:20.)

Chapter 6

OTHER KINDS OF PAIN THE SOUL SUFFERS IN THIS NIGHT

The Sepulcher of Dark Death

The third kind of suffering and pain that the soul endures in this state results from the fact that two other extremes meet here in one—the divine and the human. The divine is the purgative contemplation we've been discussing, and the human (the soul) is the subject. The divine assails the soul in order to renew it and this to make it divine. God is stripping it of the habitual affections and attachments of "the old man," to which it is very closely united, knit together, and conformed, which destroys and consumes its spiritual substance and absorbs it in deep and profound darkness.

As a result of this, the soul feels itself to be perishing and melting away in the presence and sight of its miseries, in a cruel spiritual death; as if it had been swallowed by a beast and felt itself being devoured in the darkness of its belly, suffering such anguish as Jonah had to endure in the belly of the sea creature: "Then Jonah prayed unto the LORD his God out of the fish's belly" (Jonah 2:1). In this sepulcher of dark death the soul must abide until the anticipated spiritual resurrection comes.

The Lamentations of Death

A description of this suffering and pain, although it transcends all description in truth, is given by David:

> "The sorrows of death compassed me, and the floods of ungodly men made me afraid. The sorrows of hell compassed me about: the snares of death prevented me" (Psalm 18:4–5).

What the sorrowful soul feels most while it is in this condition is its clear perception that God has abandoned it (or so it thinks), and in his abhorrence of this, he flings it into darkness, for it is a grave and pitiful belief to think that God has forsaken it.

David describes these feelings by saying: "Free among the dead, like the slain that lie in the grave, whom thou rememberest no more: and they are cut off from thy hand. Thou hast laid me in the lowest pit, in darkness, in the deeps. Thy wrath lieth hard upon me, and thou hast afflicted me with all thy waves" (Psalm 88:5–7). Indeed, when this purgative contemplation is most severe, the soul feels very

157

keenly the shadow of death and the lamentations of death and the pains of hell, which consist in its feeling itself to be without God, chastised and cast out, and unworthy of Him. The soul feels that God is angry with it. Even worse things are felt by the soul in this time, because it feels that this will be its condition forever.

Isolation and Abandonment

In addition, the soul feels that all creatures have forsaken it and that it is condemned by them, especially friends. That is why David wrote, "Thou hast put away mine acquaintance far from me; thou hast made me an abomination unto them: I am shut up, and I cannot come forth" (Psalm 88:8). Jonah writes in a similar vein: "For thou hadst cast me into the deep, in the midst of the seas; and the floods compassed me about: all thy billows and thy waves passed over me. Then I said, I am cast out of thy sight; yet I will look again toward thy holy temple. The waters compassed me about, even to the soul: the depth closed me round about, the weeds were wrapped about my head. I went down to the bottoms of the mountains; the earth with her bars was about me for ever: yet hast thou brought up my life from corruption, O LORD my God" (Jonah 2:3–6). God purifies the soul in this state, that it may see His temple. The bars of the earth refer to the imperfections of the soul, which have impeded it from enjoying delectable contemplation.

Deep Poverty and Wretchedness

The fourth kind of pain is caused in the soul by another excellence of this dark contemplation, which is its majesty and greatness; from which arises in the soul a consciousness of the other extreme, which is in itself—the deepest poverty and wretchedness. This is one of the worst pains it suffers during this time of purgation, for it feels within itself a profound emptiness and impoverishment of three kinds of good, which are ordained for the pleasure of the soul—the temporal, the natural, and the spiritual. It finds itself set in the midst of the evils that are contrary to these—miseries of imperfection, aridity, and emptiness of the apprehensions of the faculties and abandonment of the spirit in darkness.

Inasmuch as God here purges the soul according to the substance of its senses and its spirit, and according to the interior and exterior faculties; the soul must be in all its parts reduced to a state of emptiness, poverty, and abandonment and must be left dry, empty, and in darkness. The sensual part is purified in aridity, the faculties are purified in the emptiness of their perceptions, and the spirit is purified in thick darkness.

Dark Contemplation

All this God brings to pass by means of dark contemplation, through which the soul suffers this emptiness and the suspension of these natural supports and perceptions, which is a most difficult kind of suffering (as if a person were suspended in the air in such a way that he or she could not breathe). At the same time, however, He is purging the soul, annihilating it, emptying it or consuming it (even as fire consumes the moldiness and rust of metal). All the affections and imperfect habits which it has acquired throughout its life are being purged as well. Since these things are deeply rooted in the soul, it must go through great undoing and inward torment in addition to the poverty and emptiness we've already mentioned.

As this happens, something amazing takes place. It is described by the prophet Ezekiel who wrote, "Heap on wood, kindle the fire, consume the flesh, and spice it well, and let the bones be burned" (Ezekiel 24:10). This speaks of the pain which is suffered in the emptiness and poverty of the substance of the soul, both in the senses and the spirit. Concerning this aspect, Ezekiel says, "Then set it empty upon the coals thereof, that the brass of it may be hot, and may burn, and that the filthiness of it may be molten in it, that the scum of it may be consumed" (Ezekiel 24:11). This describes the grave suffering which the soul must endure in the purgation that is caused by the fire of contemplation. The prophet tells us that in order for the rust of the affections, which are within the soul, to be purified and destroyed, it is necessary that in a certain manner the soul itself should be annihilated and destroyed, since certain passions and imperfections have become natural to it.

Purified Like Gold in a Crucible

Because the soul is purified in this furnace like gold is purified in a crucible, it is conscious of the complete undoing of itself in its very substance together with the direst poverty. David writes the following about himself:

> "Save me, O God; for the waters are come in unto my soul. I sink in deep mire, where there is no standing: I am come into deep waters, where the floods overflow me. I am weary of my crying: my throat is dried: mine eyes fail while I wait for my God" (Psalm 69:1–3).

In this passage we see God humbling David's soul so that He will be able to exalt it afterwards. He does the same with each of us. When these feelings arise within the soul, they should be speedily stilled. When this is done, they die in a very short period of time. There are only occasional periods when the soul is conscious of the greatest intensity of these feelings. At other times, however, they are so keen that the soul seems to be seeing hell and perdition opened before it.

Chapter 7

A CONTINUATION OF THE DISCUSSION OF PAIN AND OTHER AFFLICTIONS AND CONSTRAINTS OF THE WILL

A Sudden Remembrance

The afflictions and constraints of the will are now very great, and they sometimes pierce the soul with a sudden remembrance of the evils in the midst of which it finds itself. Accompanying this remembrance is the uncertainty of ever finding a remedy for them. To this is added the remembrance of past times of prosperity. As a rule, souls who enter this night have received many consolations from God, and they have rendered many services unto Him. This causes them the greater grief in seeing that they are far removed from that happiness and are unable to enter into it.

This circumstance was described by Job, who had experienced it. He said:

> "I was at ease, but he hath broken me asunder: he hath also taken me by my neck, and shaken me to pieces, and set me up for his mark. His archers compass me round about, he cleaveth my reins asunder, and doth not spare; he poureth out my gall upon the ground. He breaketh me with breach upon breach, he runneth upon me like a giant. I have sewed sackcloth upon my skin, and defiled my horn in the dust. My face is foul with weeping, and on my eyelids is the shadow of death" (Job 16:12–16).

What Is Worked Into the Soul by This Dark Night

There are so many afflictions of this night and many scriptural passages pertaining to them, but we're not able to quote them all here. However, many clear pictures and good

161

ideas related to this night can be gained from the passages we've already alluded to. Let us now bring our exposition of the first stanza to a close by sharing what Jeremiah had to say about it:

"I am the man that hath seen affliction by the rod of his wrath. He hath led me, and brought me into darkness, but not into light. Surely against me is he turned; he turneth his hand against me all the day. My flesh and my skin hath he made old; he hath broken my bones. He hath builded against me, and compassed me with gall and travail. He hath set me in dark places, as they that be dead of old. He hath hedged me about, that I cannot get out: he hath made my chain heavy. Also when I cry and shout, he shutteth out my prayer. He hath inclosed my ways with hewn stone, he hath made my paths crooked. He was unto me as a bear lying in wait, and as a lion in secret places. He hath turned aside my ways, and pulled me in pieces: he hath made me desolate. He hath bent his bow, and set me as a mark for the arrow. He hath caused the arrows of his quiver to enter into my reins. I was a derision to all my people; and their song all the day. He hath filled me with bitterness, he hath made me drunken with wormwood. He hath also broken my teeth with gravel stones, he hath covered me with ashes. And thou hast removed my soul far off from peace: I forgat prosperity. And I said, My strength and my hope is perished from the LORD: remembering mine affliction and my misery, the wormwood and the gall. My soul hath them still in remembrance, and is humbled in me" (Lamentations 3:1–20).

The Shadow of Death

All of Jeremiah's complaints about the pains and trials of the dark night through which he is passing vividly depict the sufferings of the soul in this spiritual night and the purgation it brings about. The soul that God sets in this tempestuous and horrible night is deserving of great compassion. Although it experiences much happiness by reason of the great blessings that must arise within it on this account, God raises up profound blessings in the soul out of darkness, as Job points out, and brings to light the shadow of death.

The Psalmist writes, "Shall thy lovingkindness be declared in the grave? or thy faithfulness in destruction? Shall thy wonders be known in the dark? and thy righteousness in the land of forgetfulness?" (Psalm 88:11–12). David tells us that God's light comes to be as His darkness was. However, by reason of the dreadful pain which the soul is suffering, it has great uncertainty concerning the remedy for this pain. David points out that God set the soul in dark places like those that are dead (like the dead of the world or the dead of the age). For this reason the spirit within is in anguish and the heart is greatly troubled.

David writes, "I cried unto the LORD with my voice; with my voice unto the LORD did I make my supplication. I poured out my complaint before him; I shewed before him my trouble. When my spirit was overwhelmed within me, then thou knewest my path. In the way wherein I walked have they privily laid a snare for me" (Psalm 142:1–3). The soul suffers great pain and grief since there is added to all this (because of the solitude and abandonment caused by this dark night) the fact that the soul finds no consolation or support in any instruction nor in a spiritual master.

Though, in many ways its spiritual director may show it good reason for being comforted because of the blessings which are contained in these afflictions, it cannot believe him or her because it is so greatly absorbed and immersed in the realization of those evils wherein it sees its own miseries so clearly. It thinks that, as its director does not observe that which it sees and feels, he or she is speaking in this manner because he or she does not understand it. So, instead of comfort, the soul receives fresh affliction, since it believes that its director's advice contains no remedy for its troubles.

In truth, this is so, for until the Lord completely purges it in the manner that He wills, no means or remedy is of any service or profit for the relief of the soul's afflictions. This is all the more so because the soul is as powerless in this case as one who has been imprisoned in a dark dungeon, bound hand and foot, can neither move nor see, and cannot feel any favor from either above or below. This is the case until the spirit is humbled, softened, and purified, which enables it to grow so keen and delicate and pure that it can become one with the Spirit of God, according to the degree of union of love which His mercy is pleased to grant to it. In proportion to this, the purgation is of greater or lesser duration in the soul.

Peace and Loving Friendship with God

This dark contemplation ceases to assail the soul in the form and manner of purgation; now it assails the soul in an illuminating and loving manner. This allows the soul to go forth like one who has sprung free from a dungeon of imprisonment and, in so doing, the soul feels and experiences great sweetness and loving friendship with God, together with a ready tt of spiritual communication. This is a sign of the health which is being wrought within the soul by the said purgation and a foretaste of the abundance for which it hopes. Occasionally this is so great that the soul believes its trials to be over at last.

Spiritual things in the soul, when they are most purely spiritual, have this characteristic: if trials come to it, the soul believes that it will never escape from them and that all its blessings are now over, as we've seen in the above scriptural passages. If spiritual blessings do come, the soul believes in the same way that its troubles are now over and that blessings will never fail it. This was certainly the case with David who, when he was in the midst of trials, wrote: "In my prosperity I said, I shall never be moved" (Psalm 30:6).

A Mistaken Belief

This mistaken belief happens because the actual possession by the spirit of one of two contrary things itself makes impossible the actual possession and realization of the other contrary thing. This is not so, however, in the sensual part of the soul, because its apprehension is weak. But, as the spirit is not yet completely purged and cleansed from the affections that it has contracted from its lower part, while changing not insofar as it is spirit, it can be moved to further afflictions insofar as the affections sway it. In this way, as we see, David was afterwards moved, and he experienced many ills and afflictions, although in the time of his abundance he had thought and said that he would never be moved. Just so is it with the soul in this condition, when it sees itself moved by that abundance of spiritual blessings and, being unable to see the root of the imperfection and impurity which still remain within it, thinks that its trials are over.

A Worse Degree of Affliction

This thought, however, seldom comes to the soul, for until spiritual purification is complete and perfected, the sweet communication is very rarely so abundant as to conceal from the soul the root which remains hidden. This causes the soul to feel that it cannot completely enjoy that relief, but feels as if one of its enemies were within it and, although this enemy is as it were hushed and asleep, the soul fears that he will come to life again and attack it by playing his usual tricks against the soul. This is indeed what happens, for when the soul is most secure and least alert, it is dragged down and immersed again in another and worse degree of affliction which is more severe, darker, and more grievous than that which is past.

This new affliction will continue for a period of time, perhaps lasting even longer than at first. Once again the soul begins to believe that all its blessings are over forever. Although it had thought during its first trial that there were no more afflictions which it could suffer, and after the trials passed, it enjoyed great blessings; this experience is not sufficient to take away its belief, during this second degree of trial, that all is now over for it and that it will never again be as happy as it was in the past. This belief, of which the soul is so certain, is caused by the actual apprehension of the spirit, which annihilates within it all that is contrary to it.

Little Relief from Affliction

During this time of continued purgation, the soul continues to suffer great misgivings as to whether it will ever be free from the trials of life and whether its pains will ever be over. Although these souls have the habit of three of the theological virtues—faith, hope, and charity—the present realization which they have of their afflictions and their deprivation of God will not allow them to enjoy the present blessing and consolation provided by these virtues. Although they are able to realize that they have a great love for God, this is no consolation to them, since they cannot think that God loves them or that they are worthy of His love. Rather, they see themselves as being deprived of Him and left in their own miseries. Likewise, they think that they have within them things which provide a very good reason why they should with perfect justice be abhorred and cast out by God forever!

Although the soul that is going through this purgation is conscious that it has a great love for God and would give a thousand lives for Him (which is the truth, for in these trials such souls love their God very earnestly), yet this is no relief to it, but rather it brings the soul even greater affliction. The fact is that the soul loves God so much that it cares about nothing else. When therefore it sees itself to be so wretched that it cannot believe that God loves it, nor that there is or ever will be a reason why He should do so, the soul believes that it should be abhorred not only by God, but by all creatures forever. It is so grieved to see in itself reasons for deserving to be cast out by Him for whom it has such great love and desire.

Chapter 8

ADDITIONAL PAINS WHICH AFFLICT THE SOUL IN THIS STATE

A Cloud Passes Over

Another thing begins to afflict and distress the soul greatly as well. As this dark night has hindered its faculties and affections, it is unable to raise its affection or its mind to God. Neither can it pray to Him, thinking, as Jeremiah did concerning himself, that God has set a cloud before it through which its prayer cannot pass. Jeremiah wrote: "Thou hast covered thyself with a cloud, that our prayer should not pass through" (Lamentations 3:44).

In an earlier verse Jeremiah puts it this way: "He hath inclosed my ways with hewn stone, he hath made my paths crooked" (Lamentations 3:9). A dark cloud and a wall of stone are blocking the soul from reaching God. If it sometimes prays, it does so with a great lack of strength and sweetness, because it thinks God is not hearing it or paying any attention to it. The prophet Jeremiah knew what that felt like.

In truth, this is no time for the soul to attempt to speak with God. Rather, it should put its mouth in the dust, as Jeremiah says, in the belief that some hope may come to it. Jeremiah wrote: "He sitteth alone and keepeth silence, because he hath borne it upon him. He putteth his mouth in the dust; if so be there may be hope" (Lamentations 3:28–29). Such an attitude of humility will enable the soul to endure its purgation with patience.

God is working passively in the soul; therefore, the soul can do nothing. Hence, it can neither pray nor pay attention when it is in the presence of divine things. In a similar vein, it cannot even attend to other things and affairs, such as temporal matters. It has many distractions and much forgetfulness in its memory so that frequent periods pass by without its knowing what it has been doing or thinking or what it is going to do. Neither can it pay any attention (although it desires to do so) to anything that occupies it.

Annihilation

Not only is the understanding purged of its light and the will of its affections, but the memory is also purged of meditation and knowledge. It is well that this annihilation should come to it in these realms and all other things, as David pointed out: "Thus my heart was grieved, and I was pricked in my reins. So foolish was I, and ignorant: I was as a beast before thee" (Psalm 73:21–22). David was pricked in his reins; he was annihilated without realizing it. This unknowing refers to the follies and forgetfulness of the memory. These distractions are caused by the interior recollection wherein this contemplation absorbs the soul.

In order for the soul to be divinely prepared and tempered with its faculties for the divine union of love, it is well for it to be first of all absorbed, with all its faculties, in this divine and dark spiritual light of contemplation. Thus, it is to be withdrawn from all the affections and apprehensions

168

of the creatures, which condition ordinarily continues in proportion to its intensity. Thus, the simpler and the purer is this divine light in its assault upon the soul, the more does it darken it, void and annihilate it, according to its particular apprehensions and affections, both with regard to things above and to things below. Similarly, the less simple and pure it is in this assault, the less deprivation it causes it and the less dark it is to the soul. Yet, this may readily be understood if we consider what has been proved above by the dictum of the philosopher; namely, that the brighter and the more manifest in themselves are supernatural things, the darker they are to our understanding.

The Properties of Light

Let's make a comparison of what we are teaching here with common and natural light. We can observe that a ray of sunlight which enters through a window is less clearly visible, the purer and freer it is from specks within it. However, the more specks and motes there are in the air, the brighter the light is to the eye. The reason for this is that it is not the light itself that we are seeing. The light is but the means whereby the other things that it strikes are seen, and then it is also seen through its reflection in them. Without this phenomenon taking place, neither the light nor the specks would be seen.

Thus, if the ray of sunlight enters through the window of one room and passes out through another on the other side, traversing the room; and if it met nothing along the way, or if there were no specks in the air for it to strike, the room would have no more light than before, and the ray of light would not be visible. In fact, if we consider this carefully, there is more darkness where the ray is, since it absorbs and obscures any other light. Yet it is itself invisible because, as we have said, there are no visible objects which it can strike.

What the Divine Ray of Contemplation Does in the Soul

This is precisely what the divine ray of contemplation does in the soul. Assailing it with its divine light, it transcends the natural power of the soul, darkens it, and deprives it of all natural affections and apprehensions which it previously apprehended by means of natural light. Thus, it leaves it not only dark, but likewise empty, according to its faculties and desires, both spiritual and natural. By thus leaving it empty and in darkness, it purges and illumines it with divine spiritual light, although the soul does not think it has this light, still believing it's in darkness. This is comparable to what we said of the ray of sunlight, which although it was in the midst of the room, if it is pure and meets nothing in its path, it is invisible.

With regard to the spiritual light by which the soul is assailed, however, when it has something to strike—that is, when something spiritual presents itself to be understood, no matter how small a speck it is, whether it is of perfection or imperfection, and whether it be a judgment of the falsehood or truth of a thing—the soul then sees and understands much more clearly than before it found itself in these dark places. In exactly the same way it discerns the spiritual light which it has in order that it may readily discern the imperfection which is presented to it; even as the ray of which we have been speaking is dark and invisible within the room. If one introduces a hand or any other thing into its path, the hand is then seen and it is realized then that sunlight is present.

The Spiritual Man Searches All Things

Since this spiritual light is so simple, pure, and general, and is not appropriated or restricted to any particular thing that can be understood, whether natural or divine (since, with respect to all these apprehensions, the faculties of the soul are empty and annihilated), it follows that with great comprehensiveness and readiness, the soul discerns and

170

penetrates the things that present themselves to it, whether from above or below. The apostle Paul wrote: "But God hath revealed them unto us by his Spirit: for the Spirit searcheth all things, yea, the deep things of God" (1 Corinthians 2:10). This means that a spiritual person, with the aid of the Holy Spirit, can search all things, even the deep things of God.

This enables us to understand what the Holy Spirit is saying to us. His truth and wisdom reach wherever they will by reason of their purity. They are not restricted to any particular object of the intellect or the affections. This is characteristic of the spirit that has been purged and annihilated with respect to all particular affections and objects of the understanding. It is in this state that it has pleasure in nothing and understands nothing in particular, but it dwells in emptiness, darkness, and obscurity. It is fully prepared to embrace everything to the end that the words of Saint Paul might be fulfilled in it: "As sorrowful, yet alway rejoicing; as poor, yet making many rich; as having nothing, and yet possessing all things" (2 Corinthians 6:10). The Latin phrase for this is *nihil habentes, et omnia possidentes*. Such poverty of spirit as this deserves great happiness.

Chapter 9

HOW THIS NIGHT BRINGS DARKNESS TO THE SPIRIT IN ORDER TO ILLUMINATE IT

Light in Everything

Although this happy night brings darkness to the spirit, it does so only to give it light in everything. Although it humbles it and makes it miserable, it does so only to exalt it and to raise it up. Although it impoverishes it and empties it of all natural affection and attachment, it does so only

171

that it may enable it to stretch forward divinely, and thus experience fruitfulness in all things, both above and below. In so doing, it is able to preserve its unrestricted liberty of spirit in them all.

In the same way that the elements, in order that they may have a part in all natural entities and compounds, must have no particular color, odor, or taste, so as to be able to combine with all tastes, odors, and colors; just so must the spirit be simple, pure, and detached from all kinds of natural affection, whether habitual or actual, to the end that it may be able freely to share in the breadth of spirit of the divine wisdom, through which, in its purity, it has experience of all the sweetness of all things in a certain and preeminently excellent way. This implies a certain eminence of excellence.

Without this purgation, it will be wholly unable to feel or experience the satisfaction of all this abundance of spiritual sweetness. One single affection remaining in the spirit or one particular thing to which it clings, either actually or habitually, suffices to hinder it from feeling or experiencing or communicating the delicacy and intimate sweetness of the spirit of love, which contains within itself all sweetness to a most eminent degree.

Divine Light

This is even as the children of Israel, solely because they retained one single affection and remembrance—namely, the fleshpots and meals they had tasted in Egypt—were unable to relish the manna, the delicate bread of angels, in the desert. They even went so far as to say:

> "Would to God we had died by the hand of the LORD in the land of Egypt, when we sat by the flesh pots, and when we did eat bread to the full; for ye have brought us forth into this wilderness, to kill this whole assembly with hunger" (Exodus 16:3).

That manna, according to the Scriptures, held sweetness for every taste, and it conformed to the tastes that each one desired. Even so the spirit cannot succeed in enjoying the delights of the spirit of liberty, according to the desire of the will, if it still has affections for any desire, whether actual or habitual, or to particular objects of understanding or any other apprehension. The reason for this is that the affections, feelings, and apprehensions of the perfect spirit, being divine, are of another kind and of a very different order from those that are natural. They are preeminent, so that in order for both to actually and habitually possess the one, it is needful to expel and annihilate the other, for two contrary things cannot exist within the same person.

Therefore, it is most fitting and necessary, if the soul is to pass to these great things, that this dark night of contemplation should first of all annihilate and undo it in its meanness, bringing it into darkness, aridity, affliction, and emptiness; for the light which is to be given to it is a divine light of the highest kind. It transcends all natural light and can find no place in the understanding.

Divine Love

Thus, it is fitting that if the understanding is to be united with that light and become divine in the state of perfection, it should first of all be purged and annihilated as to its natural light. And by means of this dark contemplation it must be brought actually into darkness. This darkness should continue for as long as necessary in order to expel and annihilate the habit which the soul has long since formed in its manner of understanding. The divine light and illumination will then take its place. Thus, inasmuch as that power of understanding which it had before is natural, it follows that the darkness which it suffers here is profound and horrible and most painful. This darkness, being felt in the deepest substance of the spirit, seems to be substantial darkness indeed.

173

Similarly the affection of love which is to be given to it in the divine union of love is divine and therefore very spiritual, subtle, delicate, and very intimate. It transcends every affection and feeling of the will and every desire as well. Therefore, it is fitting that in order that the will may be able to attain to this divine affection and most lofty delight, to feel it and experience it through the union of love, it must be purged and annihilated in all its affections and feelings and be left in a condition of aridity and constraint that is proportionate to the habit of the natural affections it had before with respect to both divine and human things.

Thus, being exhausted, withered, and thoroughly tried in the fire of this dark contemplation and having driven away every kind of evil spirit, it may have a simple and pure disposition, and its palate may be purged and healthy, so that it may feel the rare and sublime touches of divine love. In this way it will see itself being divinely transformed, and all the contrariness which it used to have, whether actual or habitual, will be expelled.

A Magnificent Communion with God

Moreover, in order to attain the said union to which this dark night is disposing and leading it, the soul must be filled and endowed with a certain glorious magnificence in its communion with God. This includes innumerable blessings which spring from the delights that exceed all the abundance that the soul can naturally possess. By nature the soul is so weak and impure that it cannot receive all this. The prophet Isaiah wrote, "For since the beginning of the world men have not heard, nor perceived by the ear, neither hath the eye seen, O God, beside thee, what he hath prepared for him that waiteth for him" (Isaiah 64:4).

In light of this it is appropriate that the soul be brought into emptiness and poverty of spirit and purged from all help, consolation, and natural apprehension with respect to all things, both above and below. In this way, being empty, the soul is able to be poor in spirit and freed from "the old man" in order to live that new and blessed life which is attained by means of this night, and which is the state of union with God.

The Straitening of the Spirit

The soul is now set to attain to the possession of a sense and of a divine knowledge, which is very generous and full of sweetness with respect to things divine and human. These do fall within the common experience and natural knowledge of the soul (because it looks on them with eyes as different from those of the past as spirit is different from sense and the divine is different from the human), the spirit must be straitened and accepting of hardships, as regards its common and natural experience. It must also be brought by means of this purgative contemplation into great anguish and affliction. Likewise, the memory must be borne far from all agreeable and peaceful knowledge and have an intimate sense and feeling that it is making a pilgrimage and being a stranger to all things, so that it will seem to it that all things are strange and of a different kind from that which they were accustomed to.

This night is gradually drawing the spirit away from its ordinary and common experience of things and bringing it nearer the divine sense, which is a stranger and alien to all human ways. It seems now to the soul that it is going forth from its very self with much affliction. At other times it wonders if it is under a charm or a spell, and it goes about marveling at the things that it sees and hears, which seem very strange and rare to it, though they are the same things it was accustomed to experience beforehand. The reason for this is that the soul is now becoming alien and remote from common sense and the knowledge of things in order that, being annihilated in this respect, it may be informed with the divine, which belongs to the next life rather than this one.

The Spirit of Salvation

The soul suffers all these afflictive purgations of the spirit to the end that it may be begotten anew in spiritual life by means of the divine inflowing, and in these pangs may bring forth the spirit of salvation so that the words of Isaiah will be fulfilled: "Like as a woman with a child, that draweth near the time of her delivery, is in pain, and crieth out in her pangs; so have we been in thy sight, O LORD. We have been with child, we have been in pain, we have as it were brought forth wind; we have not wrought any deliverance in the earth; neither have the inhabitants of the world fallen" (Isaiah 26:17–18). The prophet is declaring here that the pain experienced by the soul brings forth the spirit of salvation. Moreover, by means of this contemplative night, the soul is prepared for the attainment of inward peace and tranquility, which is so delectable that, as the Scripture says, it passes all understanding. Paul wrote, "And the peace of God, which passeth all understanding, shall keep your hearts and minds through Christ Jesus" (Philippians 4:7).

It therefore behooves the soul to abandon all its former peace, which was in reality no peace at all, since it was involved in its various imperfections. It appeared to be peace to the soul, because it was following its own inclinations, which were based on a desire for peace. Indeed, it seemed to be a twofold peace. The soul believed that it had already acquired the peace of the senses and of the spirit, but it was still far from being perfect peace. The soul then must be purged of that former peace and disquieted concerning it and withdrawn from it. This is what Jeremiah refers to when he writes: "And thou hast removed my soul far off from peace: I forgat prosperity" (Lamentations 3:17). This truly was one of Jeremiah's lamentations.

Deep Sighs and Groans

This is a painful disturbance that involves many misgivings, imaginings, and strivings which take place within the soul itself. The apprehension and realization of the miseries in which it sees itself make the soul think that it is lost and that its blessings have gone forever. Therefore, the spirit experiences great pain and a sighing so deep that it results in spiritual groans and cries. Sometimes the soul even gives vocal expression to these. When it has the necessary strength and power to do so, it dissolves into tears, although this relief seldom comes to it. David describes this very aptly for us: "I am feeble and sore broken: I have roared by reason of the disquietness of my heart" (Psalm 38:8). His roaring implies great pain. The sudden and acute remembrance of the miseries wherein the soul sees itself, cause the pain and affliction to rise up and surround it. It seems almost impossible to describe this torment unless we take another look at Job who, when he was going through severe trials, uttered these words: "For my sighing cometh before I eat, and my roarings are poured out like the waters" (Job 3:24). In the same way that flood waters overwhelm and fill everything, these experiences bring an overwhelming affliction to the soul that grows to such an extent that it is completely penetrated and filled with spiritual pain and anguish in all its deep affections and energies. It is quite impossible to exaggerate the full extent of this experience.

A Pain That Tears the Soul to Pieces

Such is the work that is wrought in the soul by this night—a night so dark that it hides the hopes of the light of day. With regard to this, Job said: "My bones are pierced in me in the night season: and my sinews take no rest" (Job 30:17). Job's will is pierced with sorrows through the night, and he gets no rest. His soul is so pierced with these pains that it is literally torn to pieces. The pain does not cease, and he is unable to rest, for the doubts and misgivings which pierce the soul in this way never cease.

The Firmer the Edifice, the Harder the Labor

The warfare and striving within the soul is deep, and the peace which the soul hopes for is very deep as well. The spiritual pain is intimate and delicate, for the love which it will possess will likewise be very intimate and refined. The more intimate and the more perfect the finished work is to be and to remain, the more intimate, perfect, and pure must be the labor. The firmer the edifice, the harder the labor. This is what Job refers to in this passage: "And now my soul is poured out upon me; the days of affliction have taken hold upon me" (Job 30:16). Job is saying that his soul is fading within itself, and its vitals are being consumed without any hope!

The soul will attain to the possession and fruition of innumerable blessings, gifts, and virtues by means of the purgative night through which it must pass. It is journeying to a state of perfection. Therefore, it must see itself and feel itself withdrawn from the faculties of the soul and experience spiritual poverty over its losses. It needs to feel itself so far from them that it cannot persuade itself that it will ever reach them again.

Likewise, the soul must convince itself that all its good things are over. Jeremiah said, "And thou hast removed my soul far off from peace: I forgat prosperity" (Lamentations 3:17).

The Light of Contemplation

Let us now see the reason why this light of contemplation, which is so sweet and blessed to the soul that there is nothing more desirable (for, as has been said before, it is the same wherewith the soul must be united and wherein it must find all the good things in the state of perfection that it desires),

178

produces, when it assails the soul, these beginnings which are so painful and these effects which are so disagreeable.

The Reason for the Suffering

In contemplation and the divine inflowing there is nothing that of itself can cause affliction. Rather, they cause great sweetness and delight. The cause of the suffering is found in the weakness and imperfection from which the soul suffers, and the dispositions within itself that make it unfit to receive these divine benefits. Therefore, when the divine light assails the soul, it causes it to suffer.

Chapter 10

EXPLAINS THIS PURGATION BY WAY OF A COMPARISON

Preparation for Perfect Union

The purgative and loving knowledge or divine light acts upon the soul which it is purging and preparing for perfect union with it in the same way that fire acts upon a log of wood in order to transform it into itself. Fire acting upon wood begins to dry it out by driving out the moisture and causing it to lose the water it contains within itself. Then the fire begins to make the wood black and unsightly. At the same time it causes the wood to give off a bad odor. Then as it dries little by little, it brings out and drives away all the dark and unsightly accidents which are contrary to the nature of fire.

Finally, it begins to kindle it externally and give it heat, and at last transforms it into itself and makes it as beautiful as the fire. In this respect, the wood has neither passivity nor activity of its own, save for its weight, which is greater; and its substance, which is denser than that of fire, for it now has within itself the properties and activities of fire. Thus, it is dry and it dries. It is hot and it heats. It is bright and it gives brightness. And it is much less heavy than before. All these properties and effects are caused in it by the fire.

The Transformation of the Soul

In this same way we have to philosophize with respect to the divine fire of contemplative love which, before it unites and transforms the soul in itself, purges it of all its contrary accidents. It drives out its unsightliness and makes it black and dark so that it seems more unsightly and abominable that it had been before. The divine purgation is removing all the evil and vicious temperaments which the soul has never perceived because they were so deeply rooted and grounded in it. But now that they are to be driven forth and annihilated, these things reveal themselves and become visible to the soul, because it is so brightly illuminated by this dark night of contemplation. (It is no worse than before, however, either in itself or in its relationship with God.) As it sees within itself that which it did not see before, it becomes clear to it that not only is it unfit to be seen by God, but deserves His abhorrence, and that He does indeed abhor it. By this comparison we can now understand many things concerning the purpose for the purgation of the soul.

Light and Loving Wisdom

First, we can understand how the very light and loving wisdom, which are to be united with the soul and transform it, are the same qualities that purged and prepared the soul at the beginning. Again, this is similar to the fire that transforms the log of wood into itself, and makes it part of itself—the light and divine wisdom were working this purpose out in behalf of the soul from the beginning.

180

The Way to Be United With Wisdom

Secondly, it's important to note that these afflictions are not felt by the soul as coming from wisdom. They are felt as though they come from the weakness and imperfections which belong to the soul. Without such purgation, the soul cannot receive its divine light, sweetness and delight; even as the log of wood, when being acted upon by the fire, cannot immediately be transformed until it is made ready. This is why the soul is greatly afflicted. This statement is fully supported by the Scriptures.

The Fire of Love

Next, we learn the manner whereby the soul, as it is purged and purified by means of the fire of love, becomes ever more kindled in love in the same way that the piece of wood grows hotter in the fire. This enkindling of love, however, is not always felt by the soul, but only at times when contemplation assails it less vehemently. Then it has occasion to see and even to enjoy the work which is being wrought within it and is then revealed to it.

The worker takes his hand from the work and draws the iron out of the furnace so that something of the work which is being done may be seen. Then there is occasion for the soul to observe in itself the good which it did not see while the work was going on. In the same way, when the flame ceases to attack the wood, it is possible to see how much of it has been enkindled.

More Needs to Be Consumed by the Fire

We shall also learn from this comparison what we've already alluded to; namely, how true it is that after each of these periods of relief, the soul must go through suffering once again, more intensely than before. After that revelation has been apprehended, and after the more outward imperfections of the soul have been purified, the fire of love once again attacks that which has yet to be consumed and purified more inwardly.

The suffering of the soul now becomes more intimate, subtle, and spiritual, in proportion as the fire refines the finer, more delicate, more intimate, and more spiritual imperfections and those that are most deeply rooted in its innermost parts. And it is here, just as it is with the wood upon the fire, when it begins to penetrate it more deeply and acts with more force, fury, and vehemence in preparing its most inward parts to possess it.

Interior Rejoicing

We shall likewise learn here the reason why it seems to the soul that all its good is over and that it is full of evil. It's because nothing comes to it at this time but bitterness. In this way it is like the burning wood, which is touched by no air, nor by anything else other than the consuming fire. But when times of relief come along, the rejoicing of the soul will be more interior, because the purification has been more interior as well.

An Incomplete Joy

Although the soul has the most ample joy during these periods of relief (so much so that it sometimes thinks that its trials can never return, although it is certain that they will return promptly), it cannot fail to realize if it is aware (and at times it is made aware) of a root imperfection which remains—its joy is incomplete and a new assault seems to be threatening it. When this is so, the trial returns quickly.

Finally, that which still remains to be purged and enlightened most inwardly cannot be concealed from the soul very well in view of its experience while going through the former purification. The difference between it and that which has already been purged is clearly perceptible. When this purification assails it once more inwardly, it is no wonder if it again seems to the soul that all its good is gone, and that it never expects to experience it again. Now that it has been plunged into these most inward sufferings, all good coming from without is over—completely gone.

The Fruit of the Soul's Tears

Keeping this comparison before our eyes together with what we've already said about the first line of the first stanza concerning this dark night and its terrible properties, it will be well to leave these sad experiences of the soul and begin to speak of the fruit of its tears and their blessed properties. This leads the soul to sing the second phrase in the poem: *"Kindled in love with yearnings."*

Chapter 11

EXPLANATION OF THE SECOND LINE OF THE FIRST STANZA

HOW THE SOUL FINDS ITSELF WITH THE VEHEMENT PASSION OF DIVINE LOVE

The Enkindling of Spiritual Love in the Soul

In this phrase from the first stanza—*"Kindled in love with yearnings"*—the fire of love is described. This is something like the fire that acts upon the wood; the fire of love takes hold of the soul during this night of painful contemplation. This enkindling resembles that which we described as coming to pass in the sensual part of the soul, but it is quite different as well—as different from that other as the soul is different from the body and the spiritual is different from the sensual.

183

We're now talking about the spiritual love that is enkindled in the soul which, as it passes through these dark confines, feels itself to be keenly and sharply wounded in strong divine love. It also has a certain realization and foretaste of God, although it understands nothing definitely, for the understanding is still in darkness.

A Strong Passion of Love

At this point the spirit feels itself to be deeply and passionately in love, for this enkindling produces the passion of love. And, inasmuch as this love is infused, it is passive rather than active; thus, it begets in the soul a strong passion of love. This love has something of union with God within it and, therefore, in some degree it is able to partake of its properties, which are actions of God rather than of the soul; the actions of the soul are subdued within it passively.

What the soul does here is to give its consent; the warmth, strength, temper, and passion of love—or enkindling—belong [cling and adhere] only to the love of God, which enters increasingly into union with it. This love finds in the soul more opportunity and preparation to unite itself with it and to wound it, according as all the soul's desires are the more focused and are the more withdrawn from and disabled for the enjoyment of things.

The Strong Union of Love of God

This takes place to a great extent, as has already been said, in this dark purgation, for God has so weaned all the inclinations and caused them to be so focused that they cannot find pleasure in anything they may wish. All this is done by God to the end that, when He withdraws them and recollects them in himself, the soul may have more strength and fitness to receive this strong union of love of God, which He is now beginning to give it through this purgative way. The soul must love with great strength and with all its desires and powers, both of spirit and of the senses, which could not be if they were dispersed in the enjoyment of anything else. David wrote, "Because of his strength will I wait upon thee: for God is my defence" (Psalm 59:9). It is clear that David, by waiting upon God, is keeping the entire capacity and all the desires and energies of his faculties focused on God alone, because he knows that He is his sure defense.

A True Fulfillment of the First Commandment

In this way it can be realized in some measure how great and how strong this enkindling of love in the spirit actually is. God keeps in recollection all the energies, faculties, and desires of the soul, both of spirit and of the senses, so that all this harmony may employ its energies and virtues in this love and may thus attain to a true fulfillment of the first commandment, which sets aside nothing pertaining to man and does not exclude from this love anything that is his, but says: "And thou shalt love the LORD thy God with all thine heart, and with all thy soul, and with all thy might" (Deuteronomy 6:5).

A Hunger and Thirst for God

When all the desires and energies of the soul have been recollected in this enkindling of love, and when the soul itself has been touched and wounded in them all, and has been inspired with passion, what shall we understand the movements and digressions of all these energies and desires to be, if they find themselves enkindled and wounded with strong love and without the possession and satisfaction thereof, in darkness and doubt? They will doubtless be suffering hunger, like the dogs of which David writes: "And at evening let them return; and let them make a noise like a dog, and go round about the city. Let them wander up and down for meat, and grudge if they be not satisfied" (Psalm 59:14–15).

185

Finding no satisfaction in this love, the soul keeps howling and groaning. For the touch of this love and the divine fire dries up the spirit and enkindles its desires, in order to satisfy its thirst for this divine love, so much so that it turns upon itself a thousand times and desires God in a thousand ways and manners with the eagerness and strong desire of the appetite. David explains this well: "O GOD, thou art my God; early will I seek thee: my soul thirsteth for thee, my flesh longeth for thee in a dry and thirsty land, where no water is" (Psalm 63:1).

The Desires of the Soul in Times of Misery

It is for this reason that the soul says that is was "kindled in love with yearnings" (the second phrase in line one of "Stanzas of the Soul"). In all the things and thoughts that revolve within itself and in all the affairs and matters that present themselves to it, the soul loves in many ways and also desires and suffers in its yearnings and desires in many ways, at all times and in all places. It finds rest in nothing and feels this yearning in its enkindled wound. Job describes this experience as follows: "As a servant earnestly desireth the shadow, and as an hireling looketh for the reward of his work: so am I made to possess months of vanity, and wearisome nights are appointed to me. When I lie down, I say, When shall I arise, and the night be gone? and I am full of tossings to and fro unto the dawning of the day" (Job 7:2–4).

Everything becomes cramping to this soul; it feels it cannot live within itself. It cannot live either in Heaven or on Earth, and it is filled with grief until the darkness comes, as Job declares. He is speaking of spiritual darkness here. The soul is enduring afflictions and suffering without the consolation of a certain hope of any light and spiritual good. The yearning and the grief of this soul in this enkindling of love are greater because it is multiplied in two ways: first, by the spiritual darkness wherein it finds itself, which afflicts it with its doubts and misgivings; and then by the love of God, which enkindles and stimulates it and, with its loving wound, causes it a wondrous fear. These two kinds of suffering that are experienced during such a season are described well by the prophet Isaiah as follows: "With my soul have I desired thee in the night; yea, with my spirit within me will I seek thee early: for when thy judgments are in the earth, the inhabitants of the world will learn righteousness" (Isaiah 26:9). When the prophet speaks of desiring God "in the night," he is referring to desiring Him in times of misery.

The Dark Fire of Love

This is one kind of suffering which proceeds from this dark night, but it is accompanied with watchfulness as well—watchfulness for the Lord in the spirit until the morning comes. This is the second way of grieving in desire and yearning, which comes from love deep within the spirit—the spiritual affections. In the midst of these dark and loving afflictions the soul feels within itself a certain companionship and strength, which bears it company and greatly strengthens it so that, if this burden of grievous darkness be taken away, it often feels itself to be alone, empty, and weak. As the strength and efficacy of the soul were derived and communicated passively from the dark fire of love which assailed it, it follows that when that fire ceases to assail it, the darkness, power, and heat of love cease in the soul.

187

Chapter 12

HOW THE DIVINE WISDOM ILLUMINATES PEOPLE ON EARTH WITH THE SAME ILLUMINATION THAT PURGES AND ILLUMINATES THE ANGELS IN HEAVEN

Cleansed and Illuminated by Love

This dark night of loving fire, as it purges in the darkness, also enkindles the soul in the darkness. The spirit is purged and cleansed with the dark spiritual fire of love. They are cleansed and illuminated with love only. David wrote of this love as follows: "Create in me a clean heart, O God; and renew a right spirit within me" (Psalm 51:10). Cleanness of heart is nothing less than the love and grace of God. The clean of heart are called "blessed" by our Savior. By use of this term it is as if He is calling them "enkindled with love," since blessedness is given by nothing less than love.

Fire in the Bones

Jeremiah shows us how the soul is purged when it is illuminated with this fire of loving wisdom (for God never grants mystical wisdom without love, since love itself infuses it). He writes, "From above hath he sent fire into my bones, and it prevaileth against them: he hath spread a net for my feet, he hath turned me back: he hath made me desolate and faint all the day" (Lamentations 1:13).

David tells us that the wisdom of God is silver tried in fire: "The words of the LORD are pure words: as silver tried in a furnace of earth, purified seven times" (Psalm 12:6). Both of these men are describing the purgative fire of love. This dark contemplation infuses love and wisdom into the soul, to each one according to his capacity and need. In the process, the soul is enlightened and purged from its ignorance.

The Illumination and Purging of the Angels

The very wisdom of God which purges souls and illuminates them also purges the angels from their ignorance and gives them knowledge. It enlightens them as to those things which they did not know, flowing down from God through the first hierarchies even to the last, and then to mankind. All the works, therefore, which are done by the angels, and all their inspirations are revealed in the Scriptures, with truth and propriety, to be the work of God and of themselves. Ordinarily these inspirations come through the angels, and they receive them likewise one from another without any delay—as quickly as a ray of sunshine is communicated through many windows arranged in order.

Although it is true that the sun's ray itself passes through them all, still each one passes it on and infuses it into the next in a modified form, according to the nature of the glass. This is done with more rather than less power and brightness, according as it is nearer to the sun or farther from it.

Refined by the Fire of Love

It follows, then, that the higher spirits are nearer to God. The lower ones are purged and enlightened with a more general purification. The lowest of them will receive this illumination much less powerfully and more remotely. Hence, it follows that human beings, who are the lowest of all those to whom this loving contemplation flows down continually from God will, when God desires to give it to them, receive it after their own manner in a very limited way and with great pain.

When the light of God illuminates an angel, it enlightens and enkindles him in love since, being pure spirit, he is prepared for that infusion. But when it illuminates people, who are impure and weak, it illuminates them according to their nature. It plunges them into darkness and causes them

189

affliction and distress, as the sun does to the eye that is weak. It enkindles the soul with passionate yet afflictive love, until it is spiritualized and refined by this same fire of love. And it purifies it until it can receive with sweetness the union of this loving infusion after the manner of the angels, being now purged. Meanwhile, it receives this contemplation and loving knowledge in the constraint and yearning of love of which we are speaking here.

The Heat of Love

This enkindling and yearning of love is not always perceived by the soul. In the beginning, when this spiritual purgation commences, all this divine fire is used in drying up and making ready the wood (which is the soul) rather than in giving it heat. But as time goes on, the fire begins to give heat to the soul, and the soul then very commonly feels this enkindling and heat of love. Further, as the understanding is being more and more purged by means of this darkness, it sometimes comes to pass that this mystical and loving theology, besides enkindling the will, strikes and illuminates the other faculty also—that of the understanding—with a certain divine light and knowledge, so delectably and delicately that it aids the will in conceiving a marvelous fervor and, without any action of its own, there burns in it this divine fire of love in living flames, so that it now appears to the soul a living fire by reason of the living understanding which is given to it. It is of this that David writes so clearly: "My heart was hot within me, while I was musing the fire burned: then spake I with my tongue" (Psalm 39:3).

The Union of the Understanding and the Will

This enkindling of love, which accompanies the union of these two faculties—the understanding and the will, which are here united—is for the soul a thing of great richness and delight. It is a certain touch of the divinity and is already the

190

beginning of the perfection of the union of love for which it hopes. Now the soul attains not to this touch of so sublime a sense and love for God, until it has passed through many trials and a great part of its purgation. For the other touches, which are much lower than these and which are of ordinary occurrence, so much purgation is not needful.

The Lord Infuses as He Wills

From what we have said, it may be inferred how in these spiritual blessings, which are passively infused by God into the soul, the will may very well love even though the understanding does not comprehend. Similarly, the understanding may understand and the will love not. Since this dark night of contemplation consists of divine light and love, just as fire contains light and heat, it is not unbefitting that when this loving light is communicated, it should strike the will at times more effectively by enkindling it with love and leaving the understanding in darkness, instead of striking it with light. At other times, by enlightening it with light and giving it understanding, but leaving the will in aridity (as it is also true that the heat of the fire can be received without the light being seen, and also the light of it can be seen without the reception of the heat). This is wrought by the Lord, who infuses as He wills.

Chapter 13

OTHER DELECTABLE EFFECTS WHICH ARE WROUGHT IN THE SOUL BY THE DARK NIGHT OF CONTEMPLATION

The Presence of God Is Felt

This type of enkindling will explain to us certain of the delectable effects which this dark night of contemplation works in the soul. At certain times, as we have just seen, the soul becomes enlightened in the midst of all this darkness, and the light shines in the darkness. John writes, "And the light shineth in darkness; and the darkness comprehended it not" (John 1:5).

This mystical intelligence flows down into the understanding, and the will remains in dryness—I mean, without actual union of love—with a serenity and simplicity which are so delicate and delectable to the sense of the soul that no name can be given to them. Thus the presence of God is felt, now after one manner, and then after another.

The Touch of Love in the Will

Sometimes, too, as we have said, it wounds the will at the same time and enkindles love sublimely, tenderly, and strongly. At certain times these two faculties—the understanding and the will—are united when, the more they see, the more perfect and delicate is the purgation of the understanding. But before this state is reached, it is more usual for the touch of the enkindling love to be felt in the will than for the touch of intelligence to be felt in the understanding.

Impassioned Love

A question arises here: Why, since these two faculties are being purged together, are the enkindling and the love of purgative contemplation at first more commonly felt in the

192

will than the intelligence thereof felt in the understanding? To this it may be answered that this passive love does not now directly strike the will, for the will is free, and this enkindling of love is a passion of love rather than the free act of the will. This heat of love strikes the substance of the soul and thus moves the affections passively. And so this is called passion of love rather than a free act of the will, an act of the will being so called only insofar as it is free.

But these passions and affections subdue the will and, therefore, it is said that if the soul conceives passion with a certain affection, the will conceives passion; and this is indeed so, for in this manner the will is taken captive and loses its liberty, according as the impetus and power of its passion carry it away. Therefore, we can say that this enkindling of love is in the will; that is, it enkindles the desires of the will, and thus, as we say, this is called passion of love rather than the free work of the will. And because the receptive passion of the understanding can receive intelligence only in a detached and passive way (and this is impossible without its having been purged), therefore, until this happens, the soul feels the touch of intelligence less frequently than that of the passion of love. For it is not necessary to this end that the will should be so completely purged with respect to the passions, since these very passions help it to feel impassioned love.

The Spirit's Thirst for Love

This enkindling and thirst of love, which in this case belong to the spirit, is very different from that other which we described when we wrote about the night of the senses. Though the sense has its part here, since it fails not to participate in the labor of the spirit; yet the source and the keenness of the thirst of love is felt in the superior part of the soul—that is, within the spirit. It feels and understands what it feels and its lack of what it desires in such a way that all its affliction of sense, although greater without comparison than in the first night of the senses, is as nothing to it, because it recognizes within itself the lack of a great good which cannot be measured.

The Inebriation of Love

Here we must note that, although at the beginning, when this spiritual night commences, this enkindling of love is not felt, because this fire of love has not begun to take its hold. In place of it God gives the soul an esteem and [reverent] love of himself that is so great that, as we have already said, the greatest sufferings and trials of which it is conscious in this night are the anguished thoughts that it has lost God and the fear that He has abandoned it. Thus, we may say from the very beginning of this night, the soul is touched with yearnings of love, which is not that of estimation, but is that of enkindling. It is evident that the greatest suffering which it feels in these trials is this misgiving; for if it could be certified at that time that all is not lost and over, but that what is happening to it is for the best—as it is—and that God is not angry, it would care nothing for all these afflictions, but would rejoice to know that God is making use of them for His good pleasure.

For the love of esteem which it has for God is so great, even though it may not realize this and may be in darkness, that it would be glad, not only to suffer in this way, but even to die many times over in order to give Him satisfaction. But when once the flame has enkindled the soul, it has a desire to conceive, together with the esteem it already has for God. It has such power and energy and such yearning for Him when He communicates the heat of love to it, that with great boldness it disregards everything and ceases to pay respect to anything. Such are the power and inebriation of love and desire. It does not regard what it does, for it would do strange and unusual things in whatever way and manner that presents itself, if thereby its soul might find Him whom it loves so much.

The Power and Boldness of Love

It was for this reason that Mary Magdalene, though as greatly concerned for her own appearance as she had been before, took no heed of the multitude of men who were at the feast. She paid no attention as to whether they were of little or great importance. Neither did she think that it was unseemly or that it looked bad for her to weep and shed tears in front of the guests. Her only concern was to reach Him for love of whom her soul was already wounded and enkindled. Such is the inebriating power and boldness of love that, though she knew her Beloved to be enclosed in the sepulcher by the great sealed stone and surrounded by soldiers who were guarding Him, lest His disciples would steal Him away, she allowed none of these things to impede her, but went before daybreak with the ointments she used to anoint Him.

The Vehemence of Love

Finally, this inebriating power and yearning of love caused her to ask one whom she believed to be a gardener, a gardener that she thought might have stolen the Lord from the sepulcher, to tell her where he had laid Him, if he had indeed taken Him away. She wanted to take Him to a different place, if that was the case. She did not consider that such a question, according to independent judgment and reason, was foolish, for it was evident that if the man had stolen Jesus, he would not say so. Still less would he have allowed the Lord to be taken away.

It is a characteristic of the power and vehemence of love that all things seem possible to it, and it believes all men to be of the same mind as itself. It thinks that there is nothing wherein one may be employed or which one may seek other than that which it seeks itself, that which it loves. It believes that there is nothing else to be desired and nothing in which it may be employed, except that one thing which it believes is pursued by all.

For this reason, when the bride went out to seek her Beloved through streets and squares, thinking that all others were doing the same, she begged them that if they found Him, that they would speak to Him and let Him know that she was pining for the love of Him. The Scripture says, "I charge you, O daughters of Jerusalem, if ye find my beloved, that ye tell him, that I am sick of [from] love" (Song of Songs 5:8). Such was the power of the love that Mary Magdalene had for her Beloved that she thought that, if the gardener would tell her where he had hidden Him, she would go and take Him away, however difficult that might be for her to do.

Seeking God

This is the manner of the yearnings of love of which the soul becomes conscious when it has made some progress in this spiritual purgation. It rises up by night (that is, in this purgative darkness) according to the affections of the will. With the yearnings and vehemence of the lioness or the she-bear that goes to find her cubs when they have been taken away from her and she finds them not, does this wounded soul go forth to seek its God. For, being in darkness, it feels itself to be without Him and to be dying of love for Him. And this is that impatient love wherein the soul cannot long subsist without gaining its desire or dying. Such was Rachel's desire for her children when she said to Jacob: "Give me children, or else I die" (Genesis 30:1).

The Journey Toward Union with God

The soul which feels itself so miserable and so unworthy of God, here in this purgative darkness, has the strength and is sufficiently bold and daring enough to journey toward union with God. The reason is that, as love continually gives it strength wherewith it may love indeed, and as the property of love is to desire to be united, joined, and made equal to and like the object of its love, that it may perfect itself in love's good things; hence it comes to pass that, when this soul is not perfected in love, though not having as yet attained to union, the hunger and thirst that it has for that which it lacks (union with God) and the strength set by love in the will, which has caused it to become impassioned, make it bold and daring by reason of the enkindling of its will; although in its understanding, which is still dark and unenlightened, it feels itself to be unworthy and knows itself to be miserable.

Eyes to See God's Blessings

The divine light, which is always light to the soul, illuminates it not as soon as it strikes it, but does so afterwards. Does it cause the darkness and the trials of which we have spoken? The darkness and the other evils of which the soul is conscious when this divine light strikes it are not darkness or evils caused by the light, but they pertain to the soul itself, and the light illuminates it so that it may see them. Therefore, it does indeed receive light from the divine light, but the soul cannot see at first, by its aid, anything beyond what is nearest to it, or rather, beyond what is within it—namely, its darkness and its miseries, which it now sees through the mercy of God. These it did not see before, because this supernatural light did not illuminate it. This is the reason why at first it is conscious of nothing beyond darkness and evil; after it has been purged, however, by means of the knowledge and realization of these, it will have eyes to see the blessings of the divine light through the guidance of this light. Once all this darkness and these imperfections have been driven out of the soul, it seems that the benefits and the great blessings which the soul is gaining in this blessed night of contemplation become clearer.

Clothed Anew With the "New Man"

God grants the soul in this state the favor of purging it and healing it with this strong lye of bitter purgation, according to its spiritual and sensual parts, of all the imperfect habits and affections which it had within itself with respect to temporal and natural things as well as to sensual and spiritual things. Its inward being is darkened and voided of all these; its spiritual and sensual affections are constrained and dried up; and its natural energies are attenuated and weakened with respect to all this (a condition which it could never attain by itself).

In this way God makes it to die to all that is not naturally God, so that, once it is stripped and denuded of its former skin, He may begin to clothe it anew. Thus, its youth is renewed like the eagle's and it is clothed with the new man, which, as the Apostle Paul says, is created according to God: "That ye put off concerning the former conversation the old man, which is corrupt according to the deceitful lusts; and be renewed in the spirit of your mind; and that ye put on the new man, which after God is created in righteousness and true holiness" (Ephesians 4:22–24).

What Paul describes here is nothing but God's illumination of the understanding with supernatural light, so that it is no more a human understanding, but becomes divine through union with the divine. In the same way the will is informed with divine love, so that it is a will that is now no less than divine; nor does it love otherwise than divinely, for it is made and united in one with the divine will and love.

So also is it with the memory. Likewise, the affections and desires are all changed and converted divinely, according to God. Thus, this soul will not be a soul of Heaven—heavenly and more divine than human. All this, as we have been saying and because of what we have said, God continues to do and to work in the soul by means of this night, illuminating and enkindling it divinely with yearnings for God alone and for nothing else whatsoever. This causes the soul very justly and reasonably to add the next lines from "Stanzas of the Soul"—"... *oh, happy chance! I went forth without being observed.*"

Chapter 14

EXPLANATION OF THE LAST LINES OF THE FIRST STANZA

"I Went Forth without Being Observed,
My House Now Being at Rest."

The happy chance was the reason for which the soul speaks as follows: *"I went forth without being observed, my house now being at rest."* This metaphor is taken from one who, in order to accomplish something better, leaves his house by night, in the dark. This takes place when those who are in the house are at rest. Therefore, no one can prevent him from leaving. This soul had to go forth to perform a deed so heroic and rare—namely, to become united with its divine Beloved—and it had to leave its house, because the Beloved is found alone and in solitude. It was for this reason that the bride desired to find Him alone, saying, "O that thou wert as my brother, that sucked the breasts of my mother! when I should find thee without, I would kiss thee; yea, I should not be despised" (Song of Solomon 8:1). The bride desires to communicate her love to Him alone.

It is necessary for the enamored soul, in order to achieve its desired goal, to do likewise, by going forth at night, when all the domestics in its house are sleeping and at rest—that is, when the low operations, passions, and desires of the soul (who are the people of the household) are, because it is night, sleeping and at rest. When these are awake, they invariably hinder the soul from seeking its good, since they are opposed to its going forth in freedom. These are they of whom our Savior speaks in the Gospel of Matthew: "And a man's foes shall be they of his own household" (Matthew 10:36).

Thus, it would be fitting that their operations and motions should be put to sleep in this night, to the end that they may not hinder the soul from attaining the supernatural blessings of the union of love of God; for while these are alive and active, this cannot happen. All their work and their natural motions hinder, rather than aid, the soul's reception of the spiritual blessings of the union of love; inasmuch as all natural ability is impotent with respect to the supernatural blessings that God, by means of His own infusion, bestows upon the soul passively, secretly, and in silence. Thus, it is needful that all the faculties should receive this infusion, and that, in order to receive it, they should remain passive and not interpose their own base acts and vile inclinations.

The Perfect Love of God

Yes, it was a happy chance for this soul that on this night God should put to sleep all the domestics in its house—all the faculties, passions, affections, and desires which live in the soul, both sensually and spiritually. Thus it went forth *"without being observed"*; that is, without being hindered by these affections, etc., for they were put to sleep and mortified in the night, in the darkness of which they were left, that they might not notice or feel anything after their own low and natural manner, and might thus be unable to hinder the soul from going forth from itself and from the house of its sensuality. In this way only the soul could attain to the spiritual union of perfect love of God.

The Life of the Spirit

Oh how happy a chance this is for the soul which can free itself from the house of its own sensuality! None can understand it unless, as it seems to me, it is the soul that has experienced it. For such a soul will see clearly how wretched was the servitude in which it lay and to how many miseries it was subject when it was at the mercy of its faculties and desires, and will know how the life of the spirit is true liberty and wealth, bringing with it inestimable blessings. Some of these we shall point out as we proceed, in the following stanzas, in which it will be seen more clearly what good reason the soul has to sing of the happy chance of its passage from this dreadful night which we have been describing.

The Second Stanza

In darkness and secure, by the secret ladder, disguised—
Oh, happy chance!
In darkness and in concealment,
My house being now at rest.

Chapter 15

THE EXPOSITION OF THE SECOND STANZA

Freedom and Living Faith

In this stanza the soul still continues to sing of certain properties of the darkness of this night, reiterating how great is the happiness which came to it through them. It speaks of them in replying to a certain tacit objection, saying that it is not to be supposed that, because in this night and darkness it has passed through so many tempests of afflictions, doubts, fears, and horrors, as has been said, that it has for that reason run any risk of being lost. On the contrary, it says that in the darkness of this night it has gained itself.

In the night it has freed itself and escaped subtly from its enemies, who were continually hindering its progress. In the darkness of the night it changed its garments and disguised itself with three outfits and colors which we shall describe later, and went forth by a very secret ladder, which none in the house knew about. This ladder, as we shall observe likewise in the proper place, is living faith. By this ladder the soul went forth in such complete hiding and concealment in order to better execute its purpose, that it could not fail to be in great security; above all since in this purgative night the desires, affections, and passions of the soul are put to sleep, mortified, and quenched. When they were awake and alive, they would not have consented to this. —*In darkness and secure.*

Chapter 16

HOW THE SOUL WALKS SECURELY EVEN THOUGH IT IS IN DARKNESS

The Soul Travels Securely

The darkness which the soul describes here relates to the desires and faculties—sensual, interior, and spiritual—for all these are darkened in this night as to their natural light, so that, being purged in this respect, they may be illumined with respect to the supernatural. For the spiritual and the sensual desires are put to sleep and are mortified, so that they can experience nothing, either divine or human. The affections of the soul are oppressed and constrained, so that they can neither move nor find support in anything. The imagination is bound and can make no useful reflection. The memory is gone. The understanding is in darkness, and it is unable to understand anything. Hence, the will is likewise arid and constrained and all its faculties are void and useless. In addition to all this, a thick and heavy cloud is upon the soul, keeping it in affliction and, as it were, far away from God. It is in this kind of darkness that the soul says here it traveled "securely."

Free from All Enemies

The reason for this has been clearly explicated. Ordinarily the soul never strays, except through its desires, tastes, reflections, understanding, and affections. As a rule, it has too much or too little of these, or they vary or go astray. Hence, the soul becomes inclined to that which behooves it not. Wherefore, when all these operations and motions are hindered, it is clear that the soul is secure against being led astray by them; for it is now free, not only from itself, but from its other enemies—the world and the devil. When the affections and operations of the soul are quenched, these enemies cannot make war upon it by any other means or in any other manner.

Gaining the Virtues

It follows from this that the greater the darkness in which the soul journeys and the more completely it is voided of its natural operations, the greater is its security. As one prophet said, "Perdition comes to the soul from itself alone"—that is, from its sensual and interior desires and operations. Good, on the other hand, comes from God alone. Thus, when the soul is hindered from following the things that lead it into evil, then the blessings of union with God in its desires and faculties will come to it. God will make that union divine and celestial. Hence, at the time of this darkness, if the soul considers the matter, it will see very clearly how little its desire and its faculties are being diverted to things that are useless and harmful, and how secure it is from vainglory, pride, and presumption, along with vain and false rejoicing and many other things. It follows clearly then that by walking in darkness, not only is the soul not lost, but it has even greatly gained, since it is gaining the virtues.

Receiving, Feeling, and Tasting Divine Things

There is a question which arises here; namely, since the things of God are of themselves profitable to the soul and bring it gain and security, why does God, in this night, darken the desires and faculties with respect to these good things in such a way that the soul can no more taste of them or busy itself with them than with these other things, and indeed in some ways can do so less? The answer is that it is well for the soul to perform no operation touching spiritual things at that time and to have no pleasure in such things, because its faculties and desires are base, impure, and wholly natural. Thus, although these faculties are given the desire and interest in supernatural and divine things, they do not receive them in any way other than a base and natural manner, exactly in their own fashion.

As the philosopher says, "Whatsoever is received comes to him that receives it after the manner of the recipient." Therefore, since these natural faculties have neither purity nor strength nor capacity to receive and taste things that are supernatural after the divine manner of those things, but can do so only after their own manner, which is human and base, it is meet that its faculties be in darkness concerning these divine things as well. Thus, being weaned and purged and annihilated in this respect; first of all, they may lose that base and human way of receiving and acting, and thus all these faculties and desires of the soul may come to be prepared and tempered in such a way as to be able to receive, feel, and taste that which is divine and supernatural after a sublime and lofty manner, which is impossible if the old man did not die first of all.

From God to Man, Not From Man to God

All spiritual things, if they do not come from above and are not communicated by the Father of lights to human desire and free will (no matter how much a person may exercise his or her taste and faculties for God and no matter how much it may seem to the faculties that they are experiencing these things), will not be experienced after a divine and spiritual manner, but after a human and natural manner, just as other things are experienced. Spiritual blessings go not from man to God, but they come from God to man. With respect to this, we might explain here how there are many persons whose many tastes, affections, and the operations of their faculties are fixed upon God or upon spiritual things, and who may perhaps think that this is supernatural and spiritual, when it is perhaps no more than the most human and natural desires and actions. They regard these good things with the same disposition that they have for other things, by means of a certain natural facility which they possess for directing their desires and faculties to anything whatsoever.

Communion with God

If we are able to do so later in this book, we shall discuss certain signs which indicate when the interior actions and motions of the soul with respect to communion with God are only natural, when they are spiritual, and when they are both natural and spiritual. Suffice it to say here that, in order for the interior motions and acts of the soul to be moved divinely by God, they must first be darkened and put to sleep and hushed to rest naturally as touching all their capacities and operations, until they have no more strength.

A Great Happiness

Therefore, O spiritual soul, when you see your desire obscured, your affections arid and constrained, and your faculties bereft of their capacity for any interior exercise, do not be afflicted by this, but rather consider it a great happiness, since God is freeing you from yourself and taking the matter from your hands. With those hands, no matter how well they may serve you, you would never labor so effectively, so perfectly, and so securely (because of their clumsiness and uncleanness) as now, when God takes your hand and guides you in the darkness, as though you were blind, to an end and by a way which you do not know. You could never hope to travel with the aid of your own eyes and feet, no matter how good a walker you might be.

God Is Your Master and Guide

The reason why the soul not only travels securely when it travels thus in the darkness, but also achieves even greater gain and progress, is that usually, when the soul is receiving fresh advantage and profit, this comes by a way that it least understands; indeed, it quite commonly believes that it is losing ground. As it has never experienced that new feeling which drives it forth and dazzles it and makes it depart recklessly from its former way of life, it thinks itself to be losing ground rather than gaining and progressing, since it sees that it is losing with respect to that which it knew and enjoyed and is going by a way which it does not know and in which it finds no enjoyment.

It is like the traveler who, in order to go to new and unknown lands, takes new roads that are unknown and untried and journeys unguided by his past experience, but doubtingly and according to what others say. It is clear that such a man could not reach new countries or add to his past experiences if he did not go along new and unknown roads while abandoning those that were known to him. Exactly so is one who is learning fresh details concerning any office or art always proceeding in darkness and receiving no guidance from his original knowledge; for if he left not that behind, he would get no farther nor make any progress. In the same way, when the soul is making the most progress, it is traveling in darkness, knowing nothing. Since God, as we have said, is the Master and Guide of this blind soul, it may well and truly rejoice once it has learned to understand this, and to say, *"In darkness and secure."*

The Road of Suffering

Another reason why the soul has walked securely in this darkness is because it has been suffering. The road of suffering is more secure and even more profitable than that of fruition and action. First, because in suffering the strength of God is added to that of man, while in action and fruition the soul is practicing its own weaknesses and imperfections. Second, because in suffering the soul continues to practice and acquire the virtues and becomes purer, wiser, and more cautious.

Regaining Health

There is another and more important reason why the soul now walks in darkness and walks securely. This reason emanates from the dark light or wisdom we've been mentioning. In such a way does this dark night of contemplation absorb and immerse the soul in itself and it brings the soul nearer to God. In so doing it protects and delivers the soul from all that is not God.

This soul is undergoing a cure that will enable it to regain its health—its health being God himself who, in His majesty, restricts it to a diet and abstinence from all things and takes away its appetite for them as well. It is like a sick man who, if he is respected by those in his house, is carefully taken care of so that he may be cured. The air is not allowed to touch him and he is not even permitted to enjoy the light. He must not hear footsteps or the noises of those who are in the house, and he is given food that is very delicate in moderation—food that is nourishing rather than delectable.

Nearer to God

These particular things are for the security and safekeeping of the soul, and they are caused by this dark contemplation, because it brings the soul nearer to God. The nearer the soul approaches to Him, the blacker the darkness is which it feels and the deeper the obscurity is which comes through its weakness. This is similar to what happens when a person gets nearer to the sun. As the person draws nearer to the sun, he or she experiences greater darkness because of the weakness and impurity of his or her eyes. In the same way, the spiritual light of God gets more immense and brilliant

208

as we draw nearer to it; therefore, the more it blinds and darkens us.

Notice what David had to say about this phenomenon: "He made darkness his secret place; his pavilion round about him were dark waters and thick clouds of the skies" (Psalm 18:11). Here David is describing, by way of the dark waters and thick clouds, the dark contemplation and the divine wisdom which comes to souls. They continue to feel it is a thing which is near Him, as the Tabernacle in which He dwells, when God brings them ever nearer to himself.

Thus, that which in God is supreme light is to man the blackest darkness, as both Saint Paul and David have said in the Bible. Look at David's explanation of this: "At the brightness that was before him his thick clouds passed, hail stones and coals of fire" (Psalm 18:12). In this verse David is saying that the brightness of God's presence is covered over by clouds, hail, and coals of fire. This is to say that our natural understanding is unable to gain access to Him and His presence. Isaiah wrote: "And in that day they shall roar against them like the roaring of the sea: and if one look unto the land, behold darkness and sorrow, and the light is darkened in the heavens thereof" (Isaiah 5:30).

Walking in Darkness

Miserable is the fortune of a life that is lived in great peril and has great difficulty finding the truth. That which is most clear and true is to us most dark and doubtful; though it is the thing that is most needful for us, we flee from it. That which gives the greatest light and satisfaction to our eyes, we embrace and pursue, though it may be the worst thing for us and it may make us fall at every step. In what peril and fear do such ones live, since the very natural light of their eyes by which they have to guide themselves is the first light that dazzles them and leads them astray on the road to God!

If anyone is to know with certainty by what road they travel, they must keep their eyes closed and walk in darkness, that they may be secure from the enemies who inhabit their own house—that is, the senses and the faculties.

The Dark Waters of Protection and Security

Well hidden and well protected is the soul in these dark waters, when the soul is close to God. For as these waters serve as a tabernacle and dwelling place for God Himself, they will serve the soul in the same way by giving it perfect protection and security even though it remains in darkness. In the darkness it is hidden and protected from itself and from all evils that come from other sources. David refers to this hiding place when he writes: "Thou shalt hide them in the secret of thy presence from the pride of man: thou shalt keep them secretly in a pavilion from the strife of tongues" (Psalm 31:20). This is speaking of all kinds of protection, for to be hidden in the face of God from the disturbances of mankind is to be fortified with this dark contemplation against all the chances which may come upon the soul from others. And to be protected in His tabernacle from the contradiction of tongues is for the soul to be engulfed in these dark waters, which are the tabernacle of David that he referred to in the verse above. Wherefore, since the soul has all its desires and affections weaned and its faculties set in darkness, it is free from all imperfections which contradict the spirit, whether they come from the flesh or from other sources. In light of this, the soul may well say that it journeys on in darkness and security.

Refreshing and Fortification for the Soul

There is another reason, which is no less effectual than the last, by which we may understand how the soul journeys secretly in darkness; it is derived from the fortitude by which the soul is at once inspired in these obscure and afflictive

210

waters of God. For after all, though the waters be dark, they are nonetheless waters; therefore, they cannot but refresh and fortify the soul in that which it most needs, although this takes place in darkness and with affliction.

The soul immediately perceives in itself a genuine determination and an effectual desire to do nothing that it understands to be an offense to God and to do all it can in His service and for Him. This happens because that dark love clings to the soul, causing it a most watchful care and an inward solicitude concerning that which it must or must not do for His sake in order to please Him. It will consider and ask itself a thousand times if it has given Him any cause to be offended, and all this it will do with much greater care and solicitude than before. This stems from the yearnings of love which we already mentioned. All the desires and energies and faculties of the soul are recollected from everything else, and its effort and strength are employed in pleasing its God alone. After this manner the soul goes forth from itself and from all created things to the sweet and delectable union of love of God—*"In darkness and secure, by the secret ladder disguised."*

Chapter 17

HOW THIS DARK CONTEMPLATION IS SECRET

A Secret Ladder

Three things have to be expounded with reference to three words contained in the first phrases of Stanza 2. Two of these—"secret" and "ladder"—belong to the dark night of contemplation. The third—"disguised"—belongs to the soul by reason of the manner wherein it conducts itself in this night. As to the first, it must be known that in this line the soul describes this dark contemplation by which it goes forth to the union of love as a secret ladder, because of the two properties that belong to it—namely, its being secret and its being a ladder. We shall treat these two aspects separately as follows.

Secret Contemplation

First, it describes this dark contemplation as being secret, since, as we have indicated above, it is mystical theology, which theologians call "secret wisdom," and which, as Saint Thomas in *Summa Theologica* says, is communicated and infused into the soul through love. This happens secretly and in darkness, so as to be hidden from the work of the understanding and the other faculties. Therefore, inasmuch as the faculties do not attain to it, the Holy Spirit infuses and orders it in the soul. The bride in the Song of Solomon says this as well. This happens without either its knowledge or its understanding. Therefore, it is secret. In truth, not only does the soul not understand it, but there is no one who does, not even the devil. The Master who teaches the soul is within its substance and the devil is not permitted to be in His presence. Likewise, the natural senses and human understanding are prohibited from being there.

The Wisdom of Love

It is not for the above reason that this infusion is secret, but because of the effects it produces in the soul. It is secret not only in the darkness and afflictions of purgation when this wisdom of love purges the soul and the soul is unable to speak of it; but it is equally so afterwards in illumination, when this wisdom is communicated to it most clearly. Even then it is still so secret that the soul cannot speak of it and give it a name by which to call it. Apart from the fact that the soul has no desire to speak of it, it can find no suitable way or manner by which it is able to describe such lofty understanding and such delicate spiritual feeling. Thus, even though the soul might have a great desire to express it and might find many ways in which to describe it, it would still be secret and remain undescribed.

As that inward wisdom is so simple, so general, and so spiritual that it has not entered into the understanding wrapped or cloaked in any form or image that is subject to the senses, it follows that sense and imagination (as it has not entered through them nor has taken their form and color) cannot account for it or imagine it so as to say anything concerning it. Even so, the soul may be clearly aware that it is experiencing and partaking of that rare and delectable wisdom.

It is like those who see something unlike anything ever seen before. They might understand, however, its nature and have some experience of it, but they are still unable to give it a name or say what it is, no matter how hard they might try to do so. This happens in spite of its being a thing they had perceived with the senses. How much less, then, could they describe a thing that has not entered through the senses! The language of God has the characteristic that, since it is very intimate and spiritual in its relations with the soul, it transcends every sense and at once makes all harmony and capacity of the outward and inward senses to cease and be dumb.

The Language of God to the Soul

The Scriptures give us some very good examples of this. Jeremiah points to the incapacity of human beings to speak of God's language and describe it in words when he writes: "Then said I, Ah, Lord GOD! Behold, I cannot speak: for I am a child" (Jeremiah 1:6). After God had spoken with him, he did not know what to say, except "Ah, Lord GOD!" This interior capacity—that is, the interior sense of the imagination—and also that of the exterior sense corresponding to it, was also demonstrated in the case of Moses, when he stood before God who spoke from the burning bush: "And the angel of the LORD appeared unto him in a flame of fire out of the midst of a bush: and he looked, and, behold, the bush burned with fire, and the bush was not consumed. And Moses said, I will now turn aside, and see this great sight, why the bush is not burnt" (Exodus 3:2–3).

After this experience, Moses was not able to speak or even meditate with the interior imagination, as we see in the Book of Acts: "When Moses saw it, he wondered at the sight: and as he drew near to behold it, the voice of the Lord came unto him, saying, I am the God of thy fathers, the God of Abraham, and the God of Isaac, and the God of Jacob. Then Moses trembled, and durst not behold. Then said the Lord to him, Put off thy shoes from thy feet: for the place where thou standest is holy ground" (Acts 7:31–33).

It must have seemed to Moses that his imagination was very far away and was mute. It was unable to express any part of that which he understood about God, and did not even have the capacity to receive anything from Him. Inasmuch therefore as the wisdom of this contemplation is the language of God to the soul, addressed by pure spirit to pure spirit, nothing that is less than spirit, such as the senses, can perceive it; and thus to them it is secret, and they do not know it and cannot say it. Likewise, they have no desire to do so, because they do not see it.

Pure Contemplation

We may deduce from this the reason why certain persons—good and fearful souls—who walk along this road and would like to give an account of their spiritual state to their spiritual director, are neither able to do so nor know how to do so. They even have a great repugnance about speaking about it, especially when their contemplation is of the purer sort, so that the soul itself is hardly conscious of it. Such persons are only able to say that they are satisfied, tranquil, and contented, and that they are conscious of the presence of God. As it seems to them, all is going well, but they cannot describe the state of their soul, nor can they say anything about it, except in the most general of terms.

It is a different matter when the experiences of the soul are of a particular kind, such as visions, feelings, etc., which are ordinarily received in accord with the senses or by some other method. This capacity to describe them is not in the nature of pure contemplation, which is totally indescribable, and it is for this reason that it is called "secret."

The Abyss of Wisdom

It is called "secret," likewise, because this mystical knowledge has the property of hiding the soul within itself. Besides performing its ordinary function, it sometimes absorbs the soul and engulfs it in its secret abyss in such a way that the soul clearly sees that it has been carried far away and has become remote from all others, so that it considers itself as having been placed in a most profound and vast retreat, to which no human being can attain. It's like an immense desert, which has no boundaries—a desert that is the more delectable, pleasant, and lovely because it is so secret, vast, and uninhabited. In this way the soul is raised above all temporal creatures and the more deeply does it find itself to be hidden.

This abyss of wisdom raises up and exalts the soul at this time and makes it penetrate the veins of the science of love. It not only shows it how base are all properties of humanity and the other creatures in comparison with this supreme knowledge and divine feeling. Likewise, it learns how base, defective, and inept are all the terms and words which are used in this life to express divine things and how impossible it is, in any natural way or manner, however learnedly and sublimely they may be spoken of, to be able to know and perceive them as they are, save by the illumination of this mystical theology. Thus, when by means of this illumination, the soul discerns this truth—namely, that it cannot reach it, still less explain it, by common or human language,—it rightly calls it "secret."

Supernatural Contemplation

This property of secrecy and superiority over natural capacity, which belongs to divine contemplation, belongs to it because it is supernatural and because it is a road that guides and leads the soul to the perfections of union with God; which, as they are things unknown in a human way, must be approached after a human manner by unknowing and by divine ignorance. Speaking mystically, as we are doing here, divine things and perfections are known and understood as they are not when they are being sought after and practiced, but when they have been found and practiced.

It is to this purpose that the Psalmist speaks of the road of the soul when he says to God: "The voice of thy thunder was in the heaven: the lightnings lightened the world: the earth trembled and shook. Thy way is in the sea, and thy path in the great waters, and thy footsteps are not known" (Psalm 77:18–19).

A Secret Road

All this, spiritually speaking, is to be understood in the sense of which we are speaking. The illumination of the round Earth by the lightning of God forms the enlightenments which are produced by divine contemplation in the faculties of the soul. The moving and trembling of the Earth is the painful purgation which is caused therein. To say that the way and the road of God whereby the soul journeys to Him is in the sea, as the above Psalm points out, and His footprints are in many waters, is to say that the path is a secret one—as hidden from the sense of the soul as the way of someone walking on the sea would be. Such a person's steps and footprints could neither be known nor followed. They are hidden from the senses of the body.

Similarly, the steps and footprints which God is imprinting upon the souls that He desires to bring close to himself, those He wishes to make great in union with His wisdom, also have this property—they are not known. In the Book of Job we read, "Dost thou know the balancings of the clouds, the wondrous works of him which is perfect in knowledge?" (Job 37:16). God is perfect in knowledge, and by this are understood the ways and roads by which God continually exalts souls and perfects them in His wisdom. In the above verse the clouds represent these souls of which we speak. It follows then that this contemplation which is guiding the soul to God truly is secret wisdom.

Chapter 18

HOW THIS SECRET WISDOM IS A LADDER

God is the Treasure of Happiness

It now remains to consider the second point; namely, how this secret wisdom is like a ladder. We can call this secret wisdom a ladder for many reasons. In the first place, just as people climb up to treasures, possessions, and other things that are in high places by means of a ladder, secret contemplation enables the soul to ascend and climb up to a knowledge and possession of the good things and treasures of Heaven.

The Psalmist speaks of this when he writes: "Blessed is the man whose strength is in thee: in whose heart are the ways of them. Who passing through the valley of Baca make it a well; the rain also filleth the pools. They go from strength to strength, every one of them appeareth before God" (Psalm 84:5–7). This God is the treasure of Zion, the treasure which is happiness.

Humbled, and Raised Up to God

The secret wisdom is a ladder also because, even as a ladder is used to ascend, it is also used to descend. It is the same with secret contemplation, for the same communications that it causes in the soul raise it up to God and humble it with respect to itself. Communications which are of God humble the soul and at the same time exalt it. Upon this road the way to go down is to go up and the way to go up is to go down. Those who humble themselves are exalted and those who exalt themselves are humbled. Jesus said, "For whosoever exalteth himself shall be abased; and he that humbleth himself shall be exalted" (Luke 14:11).

In the virtue of humility we find greatness, and as the soul exercises itself in humility, God enables it to mount by this ladder, that it may descend; and to make it descend, that it may be able to mount, so that this Proverb might be fulfilled: "Before destruction the heart of man is haughty, and before honour is humility" (Proverbs 18:12).

Ascending and Descending

Speaking now in a natural way, the soul that desires to consider it will be able to see how on this road (not the spiritual aspect, of which the soul is not conscious) it has to suffer many ups and downs. The prosperity which it enjoys is followed immediately by certain storms and trials, so much so in fact, that it appears to have been given a period of calm in order that it might be forewarned and strengthened against the poverty that follows. This is very much like the situation that may take place after a time of misery and torment, when abundance and calm follow. It seems to the soul as if, before celebrating that festival of abundance and calm, it has first been made to keep a vigil. This is the ordinary course and proceeding of the state of contemplation until the soul arrives at the state of quietness. It never remains in the same state for long, but is ascending and descending continually.

The Knowledge of God and of Oneself

The state of perfection, which consists in the perfect love of God and contempt for oneself, cannot exist unless the knowledge of God and the knowledge of oneself are present. Of necessity the soul has to be practiced first in the one and then in the other. At one time given to the taste of the one, that is, exaltation; and then, at another time, it is made to experience the other—that being humiliation—until it has acquired perfect habits. It is then that the ascending and descending referred to above will cease, because the soul will have attained to God and will have become untied with Him. This takes place at the summit of the ladder, for the ladder leans and rests upon Him.

This ladder of contemplation, which, as we have said, comes down from God, is prefigured by that ladder which Jacob saw as he slept—a ladder on which angels from Heaven were ascending and descending from God to man and from man to God. God himself was leaning upon the end of the ladder. The Bible says, "And he [Jacob] dreamed, and behold a ladder set up on the earth, and the top of it reached to heaven: and behold the angels of God ascending and descending on it" (Genesis 28:12). This took place at night while Jacob was sleeping, and this shows how secret the road and ascent to God actually is. This is so different from human knowledge, for to the human way of thinking, to be ever losing oneself and becoming as nothing [annihilating oneself] is considered one of the worst possible things. It is a thing of little value in the minds of most people. But it is considered the best thing for the soul who seeks to find consolation and sweetness, which are acquired by losing rather than gaining.

Love Unites the Soul with God

Speaking now more substantially and properly of the ladder of secret contemplation, we shall observe that the principal characteristic of contemplation is that it is the science of love. This, as we have said, is an infused and loving knowledge of God, which enlightens the soul and at the same time enkindles it with love, until it is raised up step by step unto God its Creator. It is love alone that unites and joins the soul with God. To the end that this may be seen more clearly, we shall here indicate the steps of this "divine ladder" one by one, pointing out briefly the marks and effects of each, so that the soul may conjecture hereby on which of them it is standing. We shall therefore distinguish them by their effects, as do Saint Bernard and Saint Thomas. To know these effects in themselves is not possible in the natural manner, inasmuch as this ladder of love is, as we have said, so secret that God alone is the One who measures and weighs it.

Chapter 19

THE FIRST FIVE STEPS OF THE MYSTIC LADDER OF DIVINE LOVE

(As Explained by Saint Bernard and Saint Thomas)

Languish of the Soul

We observe then, that the steps of this ladder of love by which the soul climbs one by one, are ten in number. The first step of love causes the soul to languish, and this is to its advantage. The bride is speaking from this step of love when she says: "I charge you, O daughters of Jerusalem, if ye find my beloved, that ye tell him, that I am sick of [from] love" (Song of Solomon 5:8). This sickness, however, is not a sickness unto death, but it is for the glory of God. In this sickness the soul swoons with regard to sin and all things that are not of God. It does so for God's sake alone, as David testified: "Hear me speedily, O LORD: my spirit faileth: hide not thy face from me, lest I be like unto them that go down into the pit" (Psalm 143:7). Here we see David's spirit swooning away with respect to all things, including God's salvation.

A person who is in love acts in many ways like a sick man who loses his appetite and taste for all food, and whose color changes. The soul does not fall into this "sickness" if excess of heat or rain is not communicated to it from above, as David pointed out: "Thou, O God, didst send a plentiful rain, whereby thou didst confirm thine inheritance, when it was weary" (Psalm 68:9).

The sickness and swooning to all things is the beginning and the first step on the road to God that we have already described when we were speaking of the annihilation wherein the soul finds itself when it begins to climb this ladder of contemplative purgation. At this time it can find no pleasure, support, consolation, or abiding place in anything whatsoever. From this step, therefore, it begins to climb to the second step.

Seeking God without Ceasing

The second step causes the soul to seek God without ceasing. Therefore, when the bride says that she sought Him by night upon her bed (when she had fainted according to the first step of love) and found Him not, she said, "I will rise now, and go about the city in the streets, and in the broad ways I will seek him whom my soul loveth: I sought him, but I found him not" (Song of Solomon 3:2). The soul seeks its Beloved without ceasing. The Psalmist gives us good counsel on this: "Seek the LORD, and his strength; seek his face evermore" (Psalm 105:4).

Like the bride above who, having asked the watchman about Him, passed on at once and left them; similarly, Mary Magdalene did not even notice the angels at the sepulcher. (See John 20.) On this second step the soul now walks very anxiously, because it seeks the Beloved in all things. It is always thinking about its Beloved. Whenever it speaks, it speaks of its Beloved. When it eats, when it sleeps, when it watches, and when it does anything at all, its total care is focused on its Beloved. (This stems from *"the yearnings of love"* to which we referred earlier.)

Now, as love begins to recover its health and find new strength in the love found on this second step, it begins at once to climb to the third by means of a certain degree of purgation in the night, which produces the following effects in the soul.

How Much Is Due to God

The third step of the ladder of love is that which causes the soul to work, and it gives the soul a fervor so that it will not fail. The Psalmist said, "Praise ye the LORD. Blessed is the man that feareth the LORD, that delighteth greatly in his commandments" (Psalm 112:1). Fear in this context is the son of love and it causes the soul to possess eagerness to labor. What will be done by love itself? On this step the soul considers great works that are undertaken for the Beloved as being small, many things as being few, and the long time for which it serves Him as being short, because of the burning love in which it finds itself.

In a similar way Jacob, even though after he had labored for seven years, and discovered that he had to labor seven more years in order to get his beloved, to him those fourteen years seemed like a short time because of the greatness of his love for her. The Bible says, "And Jacob served seven years for Rachel; and they seemed unto him but a few days, for the love he had to her" (Genesis 29:20). Now if the love of a mere creature could accomplish so much in Jacob, what will love of the Creator be able to do when, on this third step, love takes possession of the soul? For the great love the soul bears to God, it suffers great pains and afflictions because of the little that it does for Him. If it were lawful for it to be destroyed a thousand times for Him, it would be comforted. For this reason the soul feels that it is useless in all that it does, and it thinks itself to be living in vain.

Another wondrous effect produced in the soul on this step is that it considers itself as being most certainly worse than all other souls. Why? First, because love is continually teaching it how much is due to God [how much God deserves]. Secondly, because of the works it does for God, all are perceived by it to be faulty and imperfect, and the soul finds itself in a state of confusion and affliction. This happens because it realizes in how lowly a manner it is working for God, who is so highly exalted and so majestic. On this third step the soul is very far from vainglory or presumption and from condemning others as well. These anxious effects, along with many others like them, are produced in the soul by this third step. Through this it gains courage and strength in order to climb to the fourth step.

Suffering without Weariness

The fourth step of this ladder of love causes habitual suffering in the soul because of the Beloved, but this is a suffering without weariness. As Saint Augustine has said, love makes all things that are great, grievous, and burdensome to be almost nothing. It was from step four that the bride was speaking when, in her desire to reach the last step, she said to the Spouse: "Set me as a seal upon thine heart, as a seal upon thine arm: for love is strong as death; jealousy is cruel as the grave: the coals thereof are coals of fire, which hath a most vehement flame" (Song of Solomon 8:6).

The spirit here has so much strength that it has subjected the flesh and takes as little account of it as does the tree takes of one of its leaves. In no way does the soul here seek its own consolation or pleasure in God or anything else. It does not desire or seek to pray to God for favors either, for it sees clearly that it has already received enough of these, and all its anxiety is set upon the manner in which it will be able to do something that is pleasing to God. Its great desire is to render Him some service in return for what it has received from Him.

The soul says in its heart and spirit: "Ah, my God and Lord! How many there are who go to seek in Thee their own consolation and pleasure, and they desire Thee to grant them favors and gifts; but those who long to do Thee pleasure and to give Thee something at their cost, setting their own interests last, are very few. The failure, my God, is not in Thy unwillingness to grant us new favors, but in our neglect to use those that we have received in Thy service alone, in order to constrain Thee to grant them to us continually." Exceedingly lofty is this step of love; for as the soul goes ever after God with love so true, imbued with the spirit of suffering for His sake, His Majesty oftentimes and quite habitually grants it joy and visits it sweetly and delectably in the spirit.

The boundless love of Christ the Word cannot suffer the afflictions of His lover without succoring him or her. This He has affirmed through the prophet Jeremiah who wrote: "Go and cry in the ears of Jerusalem, saying, Thus saith the LORD; I remember thee, the kindness of thy youth, the love of thine espousals, when thou wentest after me in the wilderness, in a land that was not sown" (Jeremiah 2:2). Speaking spiritually, this denotes the detachment which the soul now has interiorly from every creature, so that it rests not and nowhere finds quietness. This fourth step enkindles the soul and makes it burn in such desire for God that it causes it to climb to the fifth step.

The Vehemence of the Lover to Comprehend the Beloved

The fifth step of this ladder of love makes the soul desire and long for God impatiently. On this step the vehemence of the lover to comprehend the Beloved and be united with Him is such that every delay, however brief, becomes very long, wearisome, and oppressive to it, and it continually believes itself to be finding the Beloved. When it sees its desire frustrated (which happens almost every moment), it swoons away with its yearning, as the Psalmist says while speaking these words from the fifth step: "My soul longeth, yea, even fainteth for the courts of the LORD: my heart and my flesh crieth out for the living God" (Psalm 84:2). On this step the lover needs to see that which he or she loves, or else he or she must die! It was at this step that Rachel, who longed for children, said this to her husband Jacob: "Give me children, or else I die" (Genesis 30:1). It is on this step that people suffer like dogs, going about and surrounding the city of God. This step is one of hunger where the soul is nourished upon love. Even as its hunger, so is its abundance, so that it rises to the sixth step, which produces the following effects.

Chapter 20

THE REMAINING FIVES STEPS OF THE MYSTIC LADDER OF DIVINE LOVE

Hope in God

On this sixth step the soul runs swiftly to God and touches Him again and again. It runs without fainting because it has great hope. Here the love that has made it strong makes it fly swiftly. Isaiah wrote about this step as follows: "But they that wait upon the LORD shall renew their strength; they shall mount up with wings as eagles; they shall run, and not be weary; and they shall walk, and not faint" (Isaiah 40:31). This is different, as you see, from the fifth step.

The Psalmist puts it this way: "As the hart panteth after the water brooks, so panteth my soul after thee, O God" (Psalm 42:1). The hart (a deer) in its thirst runs to the waters with great swiftness. The cause for this swiftness is that its love is greatly increased. The soul is almost wholly purified at this point, as we read in another Psalm: "They run and prepare themselves without my fault: awake to help me, and behold" (Psalm 59:4). This is echoed in another Psalm: "I will run the way of thy commandments, when thou shalt enlarge my heart" (Psalm 119:32). Thus, from this sixth step the soul at once climbs to the seventh.

Vehement Boldness

The seventh step of this ladder makes the soul become vehement in its boldness. Here love does not employ its judgment in order to hope, and it does not take counsel so that it may draw back. Likewise, shame cannot restrain it. The favor which God grants to the soul here causes it to become vehement in its boldness. This is what the apostle

Paul means when he writes: "[Charity] beareth all things, believeth all things, hopeth all things, endureth all things" (1 Corinthians 13:7).

It was of this step that Moses spoke when he entreated God to pardon the people, and if not, to blot out his name from the Book of Life: "And Moses returned unto the LORD, and said, Oh, this people have sinned a great sin, and have made them gods of gold. Yet now, if thou wilt forgive their sin—; and if not, blot me, I pray thee, out of thy book which thou hast written" (Exodus 32:31–32). Men like these obtain from God that which they beg of Him with desire. David wrote: "Delight thyself also in the LORD; and he shall give thee the desires of thine heart" (Psalm 37:4).

It was on this step that the bride grew bold and said, "Let him kiss me with the kisses of his mouth: for thy love is better than wine" (Song of Solomon 1:2). It is not lawful, however, for the soul to aspire boldly to this step, unless it feels the interior favor of the King's scepter extended to it, lest it would perchance fall from the other steps on which it has mounted up to this point, and wherein it must ever possess itself in humility. From this daring and power which God grants to the soul on the seventh step, so that it may be bold with God in the vehemence of love, we go on to the eighth step, where it takes the Beloved captive and is united with Him.

"I Will Not Let Him Go!"

The eighth step of love causes the soul to seize Him and hold Him fast without letting Him go, even as the bride did, as follows: "It was but a little that I passed from them, but I found him whom my soul loveth: I held him, and would not let him go, until I had brought him into my mother's house, and into the chamber of her that conceived me" (Song of Solomon 3:4). It is on this step of union that the soul satisfies its desire, but not continuously. Certain souls climb a part of the way and then lose their hold, for if this state were to continue, it would be glory itself in this life. Thus, the soul remains therein for very short periods of time. God sent a command to the prophet Daniel to remain on this step, because he was a man of desires: "And he said unto me, O Daniel, a man greatly beloved, understand the words that I speak unto thee, and stand upright: for unto thee am I now sent. And when he had spoken this word unto me, I stood trembling" (Daniel 10:11). Let's now proceed to the ninth step, which is that of souls who are now perfect.

Burning With Sweetness

The ninth step of love makes the soul burn with sweetness. This step is that of the perfect, who now burn sweetly in God. This sweet and delectable ardor is caused in them by the Holy Spirit by reason of the union which they have with God. Concerning the apostles, Saint Gregory said that when the Holy Spirit came upon them visibly, they burned inwardly and sweetly through love. Of the good things and riches of God which the soul enjoys on this step we cannot speak, for if many books were to be written concerning them, the greater part would remain untold. Let's go on to the tenth step of the ladder now.

Assimilated in God

The tenth and last step of this secret ladder of love causes the soul to become wholly assimilated in God by reason of the clear and immediate vision of God which it then possesses. Having ascended to the ninth step, the soul goes forth from the flesh. These souls, who are few in number, have been wholly purged by love. Jesus said, "Blessed are the pure in heart: for they shall see God" (Matthew 5:8). This vision is the cause of the perfect likeness of the soul to God, for as Saint John says, "Beloved, now are we the sons of God, and it doth not appear what we shall be: but we know that, when he shall appear, we shall be like him; for we shall see him as he is" (1 John 3:2). This is not because the soul will have the capacity of God, for that is impossible; but because all that it is will become like God, for which cause it will be called.

A Clear Vision

This is the secret ladder, although on these higher steps it is no longer secret to the soul. Much is revealed to it by love, through the great effects which love produces in it. On this last step of clear vision, which is the last step of the ladder against which God leans, there is nothing that is hidden from the soul because it has been completely assimilated in God. Our Savior says, "And in that day ye shall ask me nothing, Verily, verily, I say unto you, Whatsoever ye shall ask the Father in my name, he will give it you" (John 16:23).

Until that day, however, no matter how high a soul may climb, there will still be things that are hidden from it; namely, all that it lacks for total assimilation into the divine essence. After this manner, by this mystical theology and secret love, the soul continues to rise above all things and even above itself. It continues to climb upward to God, for love is like fire, which ever rises upward with the desire to be absorbed in the center of its sphere.

Chapter 21

EXPLANATION OF THE WORD "DISGUISED"
AND A DESCRIPTION OF THE
COLORS OF THE DISGUISE OF THE SOUL
IN THIS DARK NIGHT

In Disguise

Now that we have explained the reasons why the soul called this contemplation *"a secret ladder,"* it now remains for us to explain the word *"disguised."* In this chapter, therefore, we will examine the reason why the soul says that it went forth by this secret ladder *"in disguise."*

The Will and Purpose of the Heart

For the understanding of this it must be known that to disguise oneself is nothing other than hiding and covering oneself beneath another garb and figure than one's own— sometimes in order to show forth, under that garb or figure, the will and purpose which is in the heart to gain the grace and will of one who is greatly loved. At other times it is to hide oneself from one's rivals and thus to accomplish one's purpose more effectively. At such times these persons assume the garments and cover which best represent and indicate the affection of their heart and which best conceal them from all rivals.

The Colors of the Disguise

The soul, then, touched with the love of Christ, its Spouse, and longing to attain to His grace and to gain His goodwill, goes forth here in a disguise that most vividly represents the affections of its spirit and which will protect it most securely on its journey from its adversaries and enemies—the devil, the world, and the flesh. Thus, the garb it wears has three chief colors—white, green, and purple—the colors that denote

230

the three theological virtues: faith, hope, and charity. It is by these that the soul will not only gain the grace and goodwill of its Beloved, but it will travel in security and complete protection from its three enemies. Faith is an inward tunic of whiteness so pure that it completely dazzles the eyes of the understanding. Thus, when the soul journeys in its vestment of faith, the devil can neither see it nor succeed in harming it, since it is well-protected by faith—much more so than all the other virtues—against the devil, who is at once the strongest and the most cunning of enemies.

The Vestment of Faith

Saint Peter could find no better protection than faith to save him from the devil, when he said: "Be sober, be vigilant; because your adversary the devil, as a roaring lion, walketh about, seeking whom he may devour: whom resist stedfast in the faith, knowing that the same afflictions are accomplished in your brethren that are in the world" (1 Peter 5:8–9). In order to gain the grace of the Beloved and union with Him, the soul cannot put on a better vest [undershirt] and tunic to serve as the beginning of the other vestments of the virtues than this white garment of faith, for without it, as the Scripture says, it is impossible to please God: "But without faith it is impossible to please him: for he that cometh to God must believe that he is, and that he is a rewarder of them that diligently seek him" (Hebrews 11:6). In fact, faith makes it impossible not to please Him. It is as if God is saying to the soul, "If thou desirest, O soul, to be united and betrothed to Me, thou must come inwardly clad in faith."

Faith Is Proven by Trials

This white garment of faith was worn by the soul on its going forth from this dark night, when, walking in interior constraint and darkness, as we have said before, it received no aid in the form of light from its understanding. Neither did it receive aid from above, since Heaven seemed to be closed to it and God seemed hidden from it. Neither did it receive aid from below, since those who taught it did not satisfy it. It suffered with constancy and persevered, passing through those trials without fainting or failing the Beloved, who in trials and tribulations proves the faith of His bride. This is so that afterwards she may truly repeat David's words: "Concerning the works of men, by the word of thy lips I have kept me from the paths of the destroyer" (Psalm 17:4).

Living Hope in God

Next, over this white tunic of faith the soul now puts on the second color, which is a green vestment. By this, as we said, is signified the virtue of hope, wherewith, as in the first case, the soul is delivered and protected from the second enemy, which is the world. This green color of living hope in God gives the soul such ardor, courage, and aspiration for the things of eternal life that, by comparison with what it hopes for therein, all things of the world seem to it to be, as in truth they are, dry and faded and dead—things of no worth whatsoever. The soul now divests and strips itself of all these worldly vestments and garments, setting its heart upon nothing in the world and hoping for nothing, whether of that which is or of that which is to be, but living clad only in the hope of eternal life. Therefore, when the heart is thus lifted above the world, not only can the world neither touch the heart nor lay hold on it, but it cannot even come within sight of it.

The Helmet of Salvation

Thus, in this green disguise, the soul journeys in complete security from the second enemy—the world. Saint Paul speaks of hope as being the helmet of salvation: "But let us, who are of the day, be sober, putting on the breastplate of faith and love; and for an helmet, the hope of salvation"

(1 Thessalonians 5:8). Here we see that hope is a piece of armor that protects the whole head and covers it so that the only thing that remains uncovered is a visor through which it may look. Hope has the property of covering all the senses of the head and the soul, so that there is nothing whatsoever pertaining to the world in which they can be immersed, and there is no opening through which any arrow from the world can wound them.

It has a visor, however, which the soul is permitted to use so that its eyes may look upward, but nowhere else. This is the function which hope habitually performs in the soul, namely, the directing of its eyes upward to look at God alone, even as David declared: "Mine eyes are ever toward the LORD; for he shall pluck my feet out of the net" (Psalm 25:15). He hoped for no good thing elsewhere.

The Importunity of Hope

For this reason, because of the green vestment (since the soul is ever looking to God and sets its eyes on nothing else and is not pleased with anything except Him alone), the Beloved has such great pleasure with the soul that it is true to say that the soul obtains from Him as much as it hopes for from Him. Wherefore the spouse in the Song of Solomon tells the bride: "Thou hast ravished my heart, my sister, my spouse; thou hast ravished my heart with one of thine eyes, with one chain of thy neck" (Song of Solomon 4:9). Without the green vestment of hope in God alone it would be impossible for the soul to go forth to encompass this loving achievement, for it would have no success, since that which moves and conquers is the importunity of hope.

Nothing but God

With this vestment of hope the soul journeys in disguise through this secret and dark night of which we have spoken, for it is so completely devoid of every possession and support that it fixes its eyes and its care upon nothing but God, putting its mouth in the dust, so to speak, as Jeremiah describes: "He putteth his mouth in the dust; if so be there may be hope" (Lamentations 3:29).

Love Leads the Soul Onward

Over the white and green vestments, as the crown and perfection of this disguise, the soul now puts on the third color, which is a splendid garment of purple. This royal color denotes the third virtue—charity, or love. This not only adds grace to the other two colors, but it causes the soul to rise to so lofty a point that it is brought near to God and becomes very beautiful and pleasing to Him, so that it is able to proclaim:

> "Because of the savour of thy good ointments thy name is as ointment poured forth, therefore do the virgins love thee. Draw me, we will run after thee: the king hath brought me into his chambers: we will be glad and rejoice in thee, we will remember thy love more than wine: the upright love thee. I am black, but comely, O ye daughters of Jerusalem, as the tents of Kedar, as the curtains of Solomon" (Song of Solomon 1:3–5).

This vestment of charity, which is that of love, causes greater love in the Beloved and not only protects the soul and hides it from the third enemy—the flesh (for where there is true love of God, the love of self and the things of the self cannot exist), and it gives worth to the other virtues, bestowing on them vigor and strength to protect the soul, and grace and beauty to please the Beloved with them. Without charity no virtue has grace before God. This is the purple which is spoken of in the Song of Solomon: "He made

234

the pillars thereof of silver, the bottom thereof of gold, the covering of it of purple, the midst thereof being paved with love, for the daughters of Jerusalem" (Song of Solomon 3:10). God inclines upon this purple covering. Clad in this purple vestment, the soul journeys when (as has been explained above regarding the first stanza) it goes forth from itself in the dark night, and from all created things, *kindled in love with yearnings,*" by this secret ladder of contemplation, to the perfect union of love of God, its beloved salvation [or health].

The Function of These Virtues

This then is the disguise which the soul says that it wears in the night of faith, while ascending the secret ladder, and these are its three colors. They constitute a most fitting preparation for the union of the soul with God, according to its three faculties, which are understanding, memory, and will. Faith voids and darkens the understanding as to all its natural intelligence, and in so doing it prepares it for union with divine wisdom. Hope voids and withdraws the memory from all creature possessions; for, as Saint Paul says, "For we are saved by hope: but hope that is seen is not hope: for what a man seeth, why doth he yet hope for?" (Romans 8:24). Thus, it withdraws the memory from that which it is capable of possessing and sets it on that for which it hopes.

For this cause hope in God alone prepares the memory purely for union with God.

Charity, in the same way, voids and annihilates the affections and desires of the will for whatever is not God and sets them upon Him alone. Thus, this virtue prepares this faculty and unites it with God through love. Since the function of these three virtues is the withdrawal of the soul from all that is less than God, their function is consequently that of joining it with God.

A Great and Happy Chance

Thus, unless the soul journeys earnestly, clad in the garments of these three virtues, it is impossible for the soul to attain to the perfection of union with God through love. Therefore, in order that the soul might attain that which it desired, which was this loving and delectable union with its Beloved, this disguise and clothing which it assumed was most necessary and convenient. Likewise, to have succeeded in thus clothing itself and persevering until it should obtain the end and aspiration which it had so much desired, which was the union of love, was a great and happy chance—*"Oh, happy chance!"*

Chapter 22

EXPLANATION OF THE THIRD PHRASE, SECOND STANZA OF "STANZAS OF THE SOUL"

"In Darkness and in Concealment"

It is very clear that it was a happy chance for this soul to go forth with such an enterprise as this, for it was its going forth that delivered it from the devil, the world, and its own sensuality. Having attained to liberty of the spirit, so precious and so greatly desired by all, it went forth from low things to high, from terrestrial levels to celestial heights, and from human to divine. Thus, it came to have its conversations in the heavens, as the soul has in this state of perfection, even as we shall go on to discuss in the following sections.

Many Precious Blessings from God

As I said in the Prologue, the purpose of my writing is to explain the dark night to many souls who pass through it and yet know nothing about it. The explanation and exposition of the poem is nearly half-completed now, although I've said much less than I might have said. Nonetheless, I've shown how many blessings the soul receives through the dark night and how happy the chance is that allows it to pass through it. Therefore, when a soul is terrified by the horror of so many trials, it is also encouraged by the certain hope of so many and such precious blessings of God as it gains therein. Furthermore, and for another reason, this was a happy chance for the soul—*"in darkness and concealment."*

Chapter 23

DESCRIPTION OF THE WONDROUS HIDING PLACE WHERE THE SOUL IS HIDDEN DURING THIS DARK NIGHT.

(Shows How the Devil Has No Entrance
to This Hiding Place)

"In concealment" means that the soul is hiding in its *"hiding place."* Thus, what it says in this phrase (namely, that it went forth *"in darkness and in concealment"*) is a more complete explanation of the great security which it describes itself as possessing in the first line of the second stanza: *"In darkness and secure."* This comes about through the dark contemplation it experiences upon the road toward union with the love of God.

Hidden From the Devil

The soul says, *"In darkness and concealment,"* meaning that, inasmuch as it made its journey in darkness, after the manner we have described, it went into hiding and found a place of concealment from the devil and from all his wiles and

237

strategies. Now the soul is truly free, because it is hidden from the devil's wiles. This came about as a result of the infused contemplation which it now possesses—an infusion that came about passively and secretly—without the knowledge of the senses and other faculties, whether interior or exterior, of the sensual part. Hence it follows that, not only does it journey in hiding and is free from the impediment which these faculties can set in its way because of natural weakness, but it is also free from the devil and his schemes. The devil, except through the faculties of the sensual part, cannot reach or know that which is in the soul, and he cannot know what is taking place within it. The more spiritual, the more interior, and the more remote from the senses is the communication, the farther does the devil fall from understanding it.

A Secret Between the Human Spirit and God

Thus, it is of great importance for the security of the soul that its inward communication with God should be of such a kind that its very senses of the lower part will remain in darkness and be without knowledge of it and not attain to it. In this way the spiritual communication will be more abundant and the weakness of its sensual part will not hinder the liberty of spirit it now enjoys. As we say, the soul journeys more securely since the devil cannot penetrate so far within it. In this way we may clearly understand the passage in which our Savior, speaking in a spiritual sense, says, "But when thou doest alms, let not thy left hand know what thy right hand doeth" (Matthew 6:3). In effect, Jesus is saying, "Don't let your left hand know that which takes place with the use of your right hand, which is the higher and spiritual part of the soul." The lower portion of your soul, which is the sensual part, may not attain to it. Therefore, it is a secret between the spirit and God alone.

A Sure Refuge

It is quite true that oftentimes, when these very intimate and secret spiritual communications are present and take place in the soul, although the devil cannot get to know of what kind and manner they are, yet the great repose and silence which some of them cause in the senses and the faculties of the sensual part make it clear to him that they are taking place and that the soul is receiving a certain blessing from them. Then, as he sees that he cannot succeed in thwarting them in the depth of the soul, he does what he can to disturb and disquiet the sensual part—that part to which he is able to attain—now by means of afflictions, then by terrors and fears, with the intent to disquiet and disturb the higher and spiritual part of the soul by this means, with respect to that blessing which it then receives and enjoys. But often, when the communication of such contemplation makes its naked assault upon the soul and exerts its strength upon it, the devil, with all his diligence, is unable to disturb it; rather, the soul receives a new and greater advantage and a more secure peace.

When the soul feels the disturbing presence of the enemy, then—wondrous thing!—without knowing how it comes to pass, and without any efforts of its own, it enters farther into its own interior depths, feeling that it is indeed being set in a sure refuge, where it perceives itself to be most completely withdrawn and hidden from the enemy. Thus, its peace and joy, which the devil is attempting to take from it, are increased; and all the fear that assails it remains without. It becomes clearly and exultingly conscious of its secure enjoyment of that quiet peace and sweetness of the hidden Spouse, which neither the world nor the devil can give it or take from it. In that state, therefore, it realizes the truth of the words of the bride about this: "Behold his bed, which is Solomon's; threescore valiant men are about it, of the valiant of Israel. They all hold swords, being expert in war: every man hath

239

his sword upon his thigh because of fear in the night" (Song of Solomon 3:7–8). The soul is conscious of this strength and peace, although it is often equally conscious that its flesh and bones are being tormented from without.

The Devil's Noise

At other times, when the spiritual communication is not made in any great measure to the spirit, but the senses have a part therein, the devil more easily succeeds in disturbing the spirit and raising a tumult within it by means of the senses with these terrors. The torment and affliction which are then caused in the spirit are great. At times they exceed all that can be expressed. When there is a naked contact of spirit with spirit, the horror is intolerable, which the evil spirit causes in the good spirit (in the soul), when its tumult reaches it. This is expressed, likewise, by the bride in the Song of Solomon, when she says that it has happened thus to her at a time when she wished to descend to interior recollection in order to have fruition of these blessings. She says: "I went down into the garden of nuts to see the fruits of the valley, and to see whether the vine flourished, and the pomegranates budded. Or ever I was aware, my soul made me like the chariots of Amminadib" (Song of Solomon 6:11–12). It was the noise of the chariots and Amminadib, who is the devil, which troubled her.

The Good Angel and the Bad

At other times it comes to pass that the devil is occasionally able to see certain favors which God is pleased to grant the soul when they are bestowed upon it through the mediation of a good angel. God allows the enemy to have knowledge of these favors partly so that he may do that which he can against them, according to the measure of justice. Thus, he may not be able to allege with truth that no opportunity for conquering the soul has been given to him. That was what he said about Job:

> "There was a man in the land of Uz, whose name was Job; and that man was perfect and upright, and one that feared God, and eschewed evil. And there were born unto him seven sons and three daughters. His substance also was seven thousand sheep, and three thousand camels, and five hundred yoke of oxen, and five hundred she asses, and a very great household; so that this man was the greatest of all the men of the east.
>
> "And his sons went and feasted in their houses, every one his day; and sent and called for their three sisters to eat and to drink with them. And it was so, when the days of their feasting were gone about, that Job sent and sanctified them, and rose up early in the morning, and offered burnt offerings according to the number of them all: for Job said, It may be that my sons have sinned, and cursed God in their hearts. Thus did Job continually.
>
> "Now there was a day when the sons of God came to present themselves before the LORD, and Satan came also among them. And the LORD said unto Satan, Whence comest thou? Then Satan answered the LORD, and said, From going to and fro in the earth, and from walking up and down in it. And the LORD said unto Satan, Hast thou considered my servant Job, that there is none like him in the earth, a perfect and an upright man, one that feareth God, and escheweth evil?
>
> "Then Satan answered the LORD, and said, Doth Job fear God for nought? Hast not thou made an hedge about him, and about his house, and about all that he hath on every side? Thou hast blessed the

work of his hands, and his substance in increased in the land. But put forth thine hand now, and touch all that he hath, and he will curse thee to thy face" (Job 1:1–11).

This would be the case if God allowed not a certain equality between the two warriors—namely, the good angel and the bad—when they strive for the soul, so that the victory of either may be of the greater worth, and the soul that is victorious and faithful in temptation may be the more abundantly rewarded.

Spiritual Warfare

We must observe, therefore, that it is for this reason that, in proportion as God is guiding the soul and communing with it, He gives the devil permission to act with it after this manner. When the soul has genuine visions by the instrumentality of the good angel (for it is by this instrumentality that they habitually come, even though Christ reveals Himself, for He scarcely ever appears in His actual person), God also gives the wicked angel permission to present false visions of this very type to the soul in such a way that the soul, which is not cautious, may easily be deceived by their outward appearance, as many souls have been. We see this in the Book of Exodus: "And the magicians did so with their enchantments, and brought up frogs upon the land of Egypt" (Exodus 8:7). It is said that all the genuine signs that Moses wrought were copied by Pharaoh's magicians. If Moses brought forth frogs, they did as well. If he turned water into blood, they did as well.

Effectual Spiritual Grace

Not only does the evil one imitate God in this type of bodily vision, but he also imitates and interferes in spiritual communications which come through the instrumentality of an angel, when he succeeds in seeing them, as the Lord said to Job: "When he raiseth up himself, the mighty are afraid: by reason of breakings they purify themselves" (Job 41:25). These, however, as they are without form and figure (for it is the nature of spirit to have no such things), he cannot imitate and counterfeit like those others which are presented under some species or figure. Thus, in order to attack the soul in the same way as that wherein it is being visited, his fearful spirit presents a similar vision in order to attack and destroy spiritual things by spiritual.

When this comes to pass, just as the good angel is about to communicate spiritual contemplation to the soul, it is impossible for the soul to shelter itself in the secrecy and hiding place of contemplation with sufficient rapidity not to be observed by the devil; and thus he appears to it and produces a certain horror and perturbation of spirit which at times is most distressing to the soul. Sometimes the soul can speedily free itself from him, so that there is not opportunity for the aforementioned horror of the evil spirit to make an impression on it; and it becomes recollected within itself, being favored to this end by the effectual spiritual grace that the good angel then communicated to it.

A Lasting Memory

At other times the devil prevails and encompasses the soul with a perturbation and horror which is a greater affliction to it than any torment in this life could ever be. For as this horrible communication passes directly from spirit to sprit, in something like nakedness and clearly distinguished from all that is corporeal, it is grievous beyond what every sense can feel. This lasts in the spirit for some time, yet not for long, for otherwise the spirit would be driven forth from the flesh by the vehement communication of the other spirit. Afterwards there remains to it the memory thereof, which is sufficient to the other spirit, causing it great affliction.

Spiritual Refinement

All that we have just described comes to pass in the soul passively, without its doing or not doing anything of itself with respect to it. But in this connection it must be known that when the good angel permits the devil to gain this advantage of assailing the soul with this spiritual horror, he does it to purify the soul and to prepare it by means of this spiritual vigil for some great spiritual favor and festival which he desires to grant to it; for he never mortifies except to give life, nor humbles except to exalt, and the life and exaltation come to the soul soon thereafter.

Then, according to the dark and horrible purgation which the soul suffered, so is the fruition that is now granted to it—a wondrous and delectable spiritual contemplation, sometimes so lofty that there is no language to describe it. But the spirit has been greatly refined by the preceding horror of the evil spirit, in order that it may be able to receive this blessing, for these spiritual visions belong to the next life rather than to this one, and when one of them is seen, it is a preparation for the next life.

Spiritual Favors from God

This is to be understood with respect to occasions when God visits the soul by the instrumentality of a good angel. The soul is not so totally in darkness and in concealment that the enemy cannot come within reach of it. When God Himself visits the soul, then the words of this line from the poem are indeed fulfilled, and it is in total darkness and in concealment from the enemy that the soul receives these spiritual favors from God. The reason for this is that as His Majesty dwells substantially in the soul, where neither angel nor devil can attain to an understanding of that which comes to pass, they cannot know the intimate and secret communications that take place there between the soul and God. These communications, since the Lord himself works them, are wholly divine and sovereign; for they are all substantial touches of divine union between the soul and God, in which the soul receives a greater blessing that in all the rest, since this is the loftiest degree of prayer that exists.

Intimacy with God

These are the touches that the bride entreated of Him in the Song of Solomon: "Let him kiss me with the kisses of his mouth: for thy love is better than wine" (Song of Solomon 1:2). This is something that takes place in such close intimacy with God, and the soul has deep yearnings for this closeness; indeed, it esteems and longs for a touch of this divinity more than all the other favors that God grants to it. After many such favors have been granted to the bride in the Song of Solomon, which she sings about so clearly, she is still not satisfied, but entreats Him for more intimacy and divine touches.

She says, "O that thou wert as my brother, that sucked the breasts of my mother! When I should find thee without, I would kiss thee; yea, I should not be despised" (Song of Solomon 8:1). The bride is speaking of the communication which God makes to her. No other creatures or entities have knowledge of this. There is an image in this verse of a suckling child (her brother); this speaks of drying up and draining the breasts of the desires and affections of the sensual part of the soul, which takes place when the soul, in intimate peace and delight, has the fruition of these blessings with liberty of spirit and without the sensual part being able to hinder it any longer. Neither can the devil thwart it in any way even though he would make bold to attack it, but he cannot reach it; nor can he understand such intimacy. These are the divine touches within the substance of the soul in the loving substance of God.

Strengthened in Union with God

To this blessing no one attains unless he or she has passed through purgation, detachment, and spiritual concealment from all other things and creatures. It comes to pass in the darkness, as we have already explained at length with respect to the third phrase of stanza two. The soul is in concealment and in hiding. It has found its hiding place and continues to be strengthened there in union with God through love. It sings, *"In darkness and in concealment."*

Wholly Spiritual

When it comes to pass that those favors are granted to the soul in concealment (that is, as we have said, in spirit only), the soul desires to see itself so far withdrawn and separated from its sensual and lower portion that it recognizes in itself two parts that are so distinct from each other that it believes that the one has nothing to do with the other. It feels that the one is very remote and far withdrawn from the other. In reality, this is very true in a certain way, for the operation is now wholly spiritual, and the soul receives no communication in its sensual part. In this way the soul gradually becomes wholly spiritual. In this hiding place of united contemplation, its spiritual desires and passions are to a great degree removed and purged away. Thus, speaking of its higher part, the soul then sings: *"My house being now at rest."*

Chapter 24

COMPLETION OF THE EXPLANATION
OF THE SECOND STANZA

In darkness and secure, by the secret ladder,
Disguised—oh, happy chance!—
In darkness and in concealment,
My house now being at rest.

"At Rest"

The last line is saying that the higher portion of the soul, like the lower portion, is now at rest with respect to its desires and faculties. The soul, therefore, says, "In light of this I was able to go forth to the divine union of the love of God. My house is now at rest—it is stilled."

Peace and Stillness

Inasmuch as, by means of that war of the dark night, as has been said, the soul is warred against and purged in two ways; namely, according to its sensual and its spiritual parts—with its senses, faculties, and passions. Likewise, after two manners; namely, according to the sensual and the spiritual, with all its faculties and desires, the soul attains to an enjoyment of peace and rest. For this reason the soul pronounces this line—*"My house now being at rest"*—in this stanza and the first, because of these two portions of the soul, the spiritual and the sensual, which, in order that they may go forth to the divine union of love, must first be reformed, ordered, and tranquilized with respect to the sensual and to the spiritual, according to the nature of the state of innocence which Adam enjoyed. And thus this line, which is in the first stanza, was understood to refer to the repose of the lower and sensual portion. In this second stanza, however, it refers to the higher and spiritual part, and it is for this reason that we have repeated it twice.

The Divine Betrothal of the Soul to the Son of God

This repose and quiet of this spiritual house is what the soul attains habitually and perfectly (insofar as the conditions of this life permit), by means of the acts of the substantial touches of divine union we have just been discussing. This divine union, in its concealment and hidden from the machinations of the enemy as well as its own lusts and passions, the soul has been receiving from God. What it has received from Him enables it to purify itself, resting, strengthening, and confirming itself in order to be able to receive the said union once and for all. This is the divine betrothal of the soul to the Son of God.

As soon as these two houses of the soul have together become tranquilized and strengthened, with all their domestics—the faculties and desires—and have put these domestics to sleep and made them to be silent with respect to all things, both above and below, this divine wisdom immediately unites itself with the soul by making a new bond of loving possession, and this is the fulfillment of many Scriptures, such as what the bride described in the Song of Solomon: "The watchmen that went about the city found me, they smote me, they wounded me; the keepers of the walls took away my veil from me" (Song of Solomon 5:7). After they smote her, wounded her, and removed her veil from her, she found Him whom she loved so deeply.

Purity Is Required

The soul cannot come to this union without great purity, and this purity is not gained without great detachment from every created thing, and sharp mortification as well. This is signified by the stripping of the bride's veil and by her being wounded by night, as she sought and went after the Spouse. The new mantle, which belonged to the betrothal, could not be put on until the old mantle had been stripped off. Therefore, anyone who refuses to go forth in the night to seek the Beloved and to be stripped of his or her own will and be mortified, but seeks Him upon his or her bed and at his or her own convenience, as the bride did, will not succeed in finding Him: "By night on my bed I sought him whom my soul loveth: I sought him, but I found him not" (Song of Solomon 3:1). This soul says of itself that it found Him by going forth in the dark, with deep yearnings of love.

The Third Stanza

In the happy night, in secret, when none saw me,
Nor I beheld aught, without light or guide,
Save that which burned in my heart.

Chapter 25

THE EXPOUNDING OF THE THIRD STANZA

Attaining the Desired Goal

The soul still continues the metaphor and similitude of temporal night in describing this, its spiritual night, and continues to sing and extol the good properties which belong to it, and which in passing through this night it found and used, to the end that it might attain its desired goal with speed and security. Of these properties it sets down three, as follows.

A Happy Night of Contemplation

The first property is that in this happy night of contemplation God leads the soul by a manner of contemplation that is so solitary and secret, so remote and far-distant from sense, that nothing pertaining to it nor any touch of created things succeeds in approaching the soul in such a was as to disturb it and detain it on the road to the union of love.

An Unimpeded Journey

The second property it speaks of pertains to the spiritual darkness of this night, in which all the faculties of the higher part of the soul are in darkness. The soul sees nothing and it looks at nothing other than God, to the end that it may reach Him, as it journeys unimpeded by obstacles of forms and figures, and of natural apprehensions, which are those that endeavor to hinder the soul from uniting with the eternal being of God.

Soaring Upward to God

The third property is that, although as it journeys, the soul is supported by no particular interior light of understanding. It has no exterior guide from whom it may receive satisfaction on this lofty road. It is completely deprived of all this by the thick darkness; yet its love alone, which burns brightly at this time, makes its heart to long for the Beloved. This love moves and guides the soul and makes it soar upward to God along the road of solitude, without it knowing how or in what manner it's happening—*"In the happy night."*

WORDS OF GOOD COUNSEL FROM SAINT JOHN OF THE CROSS

Never was fount so clear, Undimmed and bright;
From it alone, I know proceeds all light
Although 'tis night.

- If you do not learn to deny yourself, you can make no progress in perfection.
- In detachment, the spirit finds quiet and repose for coveting nothing. Nothing wearies it by elation, and nothing oppresses it by dejection, because it stands in the center of its own humility.
- The Lord measures our perfection neither by the multitude nor the magnitude of our deeds, but by the manner in which we perform them.
- I wish I could persuade spiritual persons that the way of perfection does not consist in many devices, nor in much cogitation, but in denying themselves completely and yielding themselves to suffer everything for the love of Christ. And if there is a failure in this exercise, all other methods of walking in the spiritual way are merely a beating about the bush, and profitless trifling, although a person should have very high contemplation and communion with God.

- Live in the world as if only God and your soul were in it; then your heart will never be made captive by any earthly thing.

- O you souls who wish to go on with so much safety and consolation, if you knew how pleasing to God is suffering, and how much it helps in acquiring other good things, you would never seek consolation in anything; but you would rather look upon it as a great happiness to bear the Cross of the Lord.

- In giving us His Son, His only Word, He spoke everything to us at once in this sole Word—and He has no more to say ... because what He spoke before to the prophets in parts, He has now spoken all at once by giving us the All Who Is His Son.

- Bridle your tongue and your thoughts very much; direct your affection habitually toward God, and your spirit will be divinely enkindled.

- Feed not your spirit on anything but God. Cast off concern about things, and bear peace and recollection in your heart.

- Rejoice habitually in God, who is your salvation, and reflect that it is good to suffer in any way for Him who is good.

- Crucified inwardly and outwardly with Christ, you will live in this life with fullness and satisfaction of soul and possess your soul in patience.

- Let Christ crucified be enough for you, and with Him suffer and take your rest, and hence annihilate yourself in all inward and outward things.

- The soul that walks in love neither rests nor grows tired.

- He who seeks not the cross of Christ seeks not the glory of Christ.

252

- The devil fears a soul united to God as he does God himself.
- Love consists not in feeling great things, but in having great detachment and in suffering for the Beloved.
- Speak little and do not meddle in matters about which you are not asked.
- It is a serious evil to have more regard for God's blessings than for God Himself: prayer and detachment.
- Strive to preserve your heart in peace; let no event of this world disturb it. Reflect that all must come to an end.
- Be deeply sorry for any time that is lost or that passes without your loving God.
- Whoever knows how to die in all will have life in all.
- Abandon evil, do good, and seek peace.
- He is humble who hides in his own nothingness and knows how to abandon himself to God.
- Anyone who trusts in himself is worse than the devil.
- Anyone who does not love his neighbor abhors God.
- Whoever flees prayer flees all that is good.
- Suffering for God is better than working miracles.
- O sweetest love of God, so little known, he who has found its veins is at rest!
- I didn't know You, my Lord, because I still desired to know and relish things.
- A soul enkindled with love is a gentle, meek, humble, and patient soul.
- My spirit becomes dry because it forgets to feed on You.
- In tribulation, immediately draw near to God with confidence, and you will receive strength, enlightenment, and instruction.

- Take God for your spouse and friend and walk with Him continually, and you will not sin and will learn to love, and the things you must do will work out prosperously for you.

- Be interiorly detached from all things and do not seek pleasure in any temporal thing, and your soul will concentrate on goods you do not know.

- Whoever knows how to die in all will have life in all.

- Abandon evil, do good, and seek peace.

- Conquering the tongue is better than fasting on bread and water.

References

These quotations were acquired from a variety of sources, including the following:

The Dark Night of the Soul by Saint John of the Cross.

Love's Living Flame by Saint John of the Cross.

A Spiritual Canticle of the Soul by Saint John of the Cross.

"John of the Cross," *Patron Saints Index*, http://www.catholic-forum.com/Saints/saintj23.htm

The Collected Works of St. John of the Cross. Translated by Kieran Kavanaugh, O.C.D. and Otilio Rodriguez, O.C.D. ICS Publications, Institute of Carmelite Studies, Washington, D.C., 1979.

T hough holy doctors have uncovered many mysteries and wonders, and devout souls have understood them in this earthly condition of ours, yet the greater part still remains to be unfolded by them, and even to be understood by them.

We must dig deeply in Christ. He is like a rich mine with many pockets containing treasures: however deep we dig, we will never find their end or their limit. Indeed, in every pocket new seams of fresh riches are discovered on all sides.

For this reason the apostle Paul said of Christ, "In Him are hidden all the treasures of the wisdom and knowledge of God." The soul cannot enter into these treasures, nor attain them, unless it first crosses into and enters the thicket of suffering, enduring interior and exterior labors, and unless it first receives from God very many blessings in the intellect and in the senses, and has undergone long spiritual training.

The gate that gives entry into these riches of His wisdom is the cross; because it is a narrow gate, while many seek the joys that can be gained through it, it is given to few to desire to pass through it.

GLOSSARY

Absolution – The remission of one's sins, usually pronounced by a priest of the Roman Catholic Church in the Sacrament of Penance. This absolves the sinner of his or her trespasses against God and others; it sets him or her free from the consequences of sin and guilt.

Aridity – Used often in the writings of Saint John of the Cross, aridity has to do with spiritual dryness—a figurative desert experience when one does not feel close to God and cannot appreciate spiritual things.

Anointing – In the writings of Saint John of the Cross, "anointing" is a reference to the power and provision of the Holy Spirit in a believer's life. It may also refer to a sacred rite of consecration.

Asceticism – The practice of strict self-denial as a measure of spiritual discipline. An ascetic is one who chooses a path of simplicity, devotion, austerity, and poverty. Many ascetics are mystics as well.

Avarice – One of the Seven Deadly Sins, avarice deals primarily with greed and an insatiable desire for wealth and gain. A person who is involved with this sin usually has very materialistic values.

Beatific Vision – This refers to the direct and personal knowledge of God in Heaven.

Beatitudes – Jesus set forth several Beatitudes in His Sermon on the Mount. (See Matthew 5:3–12). It represents a state of utmost bliss.

Blessedness – Extreme happiness as a result of closeness to God. Blessedness brings the bliss of Heaven to the blessed on Earth.

Calced – This is a division within the Carmelite Order of the Roman Catholic Church that has adapted the rules of the order to meet the needs of the times. (For more about the Calced Carmelites, refer to Chapter 4 of this book.)

Cardinal – A high ecclesiastical official of the Roman Catholic Church who ranks immediately below the Pope and is appointed by the Pope to assist in the administration of the church through the College of Cardinals.

Carmelites – A mendicant order of the Roman Catholic Church that had its origins early in the Middle Ages on or near Mount Carmel in Palestine. (The Order of Our Lady of Mount Carmel.) For more about the Carmelites, please refer to Chapter 4 of this book.

Carnal – This adjective deals with the flesh. It relates to bodily pleasures, such as food, sex, comfort, and luxury. A carnal person is the opposite of a spiritual person.

Concupiscence – This noun refers to ardent and eager desire for something, particularly with regard to matters related to sexuality. A concupiscent individual is filled with lust.

Confession – Within the Roman Catholic church, confession is regarded as a sacrament—the Sacrament of Penance. One confesses to a priest, and the priest absolves one of his or her sins in behalf of Christ. One may make his or her confessions directly to God, through Jesus Christ, as this verse shows: "If we confess our sins, he is faithful and just to forgive us our sins, and to cleanse us from all unrighteousness" (1 John 1:9).

Contemplation – Saint John of the Cross makes a huge distinction between meditation and contemplation. To him, meditation relates mainly to mental activity, while contemplation is much more deeply spiritual. Contemplation involves being totally focused on God and spiritual things, and it will lead to a state of mystical awareness of God and His attributes. It requires detachment, purgation, and self-denial.

Contrition – Being contrite (sorry for one's sins and shortcomings) leads to contrition. It involves true grief over sin that leads to repentance.

Corporeal – This word, like carnal, refers to the physical body and its senses. Its opposites are "spiritual," "immaterial," and "intangible."

Detachment – Saint John of the Cross refers to "detachment" often in his writings. It is a form of self-denial that makes one indifferent toward all worldly concerns, material things, self-satisfaction, or self-aggrandizement. It is a freeing of the soul that leads to spiritual happiness.

Discalced – This is a term that is given to the members of the Teresian Reform Movement within the Carmelite Order of the Roman Catholic Church. The term means "barefoot" or "shoeless," and this is a symbol of the voluntary poverty, simplicity, devotion, and detachment of discalced Carmelites who live simple and austere lives in their quest for total union with God.

Envy – One of the Seven Deadly Sins, envy has to do with a malicious attitude toward others that is caused by a strong desire to have what they have. (For more about "envy," take a good look at Chapter 8 of this book.)

Faith – One of the Seven Holy Virtues, faith involves strong belief and trust in God, which result in loyalty and devotion to Him. (For more about "faith," please refer to Chapter 8 of this book.)

Fortitude – One of the Seven Holy Virtues, fortitude involves a quality of inner strength and courage. It enables one to encounter danger or endure adversity with courage and hope. (For more about "fortitude," please see Chapter 8 of this book.)

Grace – Grace has been defined as "unmerited favor" which God extends to people, both the saved and unsaved. It enables a person to do what he or she could not do before and to be what he or she could not be before. It is a gift and virtue that comes from God. (See Ephesians 2:8–9.)

Greed – One of the Seven Deadly Sins, greed has to do with a constant desire for more of something or more of several things. It is closely akin to a materialistic addiction. A synonym for "greed" is "avarice."

Incarnation – This refers to God becoming flesh and dwelling among us. (See John 1:14.) It is a direct reference to the Lord Jesus Christ, who took on human form even though He was the Son of God. It is the union of divinity with humanity.

Lust – One of the Seven Deadly Sins, lust has to do with the passions of the body, particularly as they relate to sexuality. It involves strong and intense desire. One of its synonyms is "lasciviousness."

Meditation – Meditation, in the writings of Saint John of the Cross, is seen as something of a starting point in the spiritual life. It involves mindfulness of the things of God, but it is mainly intellectual. Therefore, it is not a spiritual exercise. It is thinking about God and His Word, and this may well lead the believer to the next step, which is contemplation.

Mortification – This noun involves death; it is the putting to death of the flesh and all its appetites and desires. It is dying to self and living for God. It involves subduing the body and the physical senses and through abstinence, pain, suffering, and torment.

Mystic, Mystical, Mysticism – A mystic is a believer who wants to always be close to God, to hear His voice, and to have an intimate relationship with Him. To be mystical is to be intensely spiritual. Saint John of the Cross and Saint Teresa of Avila were devoted mystics, who experienced mystical union with God through direct knowledge of Him, supernatural visions and revelations, and holy communion.

Omnipotent, Omnipotence – God is an omnipotent being. This means that He possesses unlimited power and might. The word literally means "all-powerful," and only God is omnipotent. He is also "omnipresent"—present everywhere and "omniscient"—all-knowing.

Penance – An act of self-deprivation, abasement, mortification, and self-denial that is related to one's devotion to God. Through penance one shows that he or she is sorrowful and repentant regarding his or her sins. It is also a sacramental rite that is practiced in the Roman Catholic Church.

Perfection – Perfection, according to Saint John of the Cross, involves total union with God. It is total freedom from all flaws, defects, and sins. It is a saintly quality of extreme excellence, purity, and holiness, and it can be attained only after one has passed through the *Dark Night of the Soul.*

Purgation – The soul experiences purgation through tribulations, trials, challenges, and temptations that are experienced in the *Dark Night of the Soul.* Through these he or she is cleansed, purified, freed from the influences of the self-life, the world, the senses, Satan, and all negative impediments to progress in the spiritual life.

Repentance – This involves turning away from sin and earnestly committing oneself to changing one's life completely. It is an earnest desire to never commit the same sins again. It involves grief and sorrow for one's sins and a complete desire to overcome them through Christ.

Seraph – A seraph is a particular kind of angel. It has six wings and stands in the presence of God in Heaven.

The seraphim are an order of angels that are sometimes dispatched to help human beings on their spiritual journey.

Transformation – This is the goal that Saint John of the Cross sets forth for all believers in his writing. It represents a total change from all forms of carnality, and it involves union with God through love. Though it won't be complete until the next life, one can experience a great measure of spiritual transformation in the here-and-now.

STUDY GUIDE

The following questions are designed to help you meditate on the life and writings of Saint John of the Cross. Some questions are simply factual/memory questions; others are application questions in which you are asked how his writing impacts your own life. There are a few interpretation questions, as well.

This material can be used for both group and individual study related to this Christian classic. Space is left after each question for you to record your answer.

EDITOR'S FOREWORD

1. What were the main influences in Saint John's life during his early years?

2. Which book of the Bible seemed to hold the greatest influence in the life of Saint John of the Cross?

3. What was the main personal goal of Saint John of the Cross?

BIOGRAPHY OF SAINT JOHN OF THE CROSS

1. What did John learn from his brother Francisco?

2. What was one of John's first jobs? How did this influence his later ministry?

3. Which nun had a great influence in John's life? How did she help him change his plans?

4. What are "discalced" Carmelites?

5. When did John take the name "John of the Cross"?

6. Why was John imprisoned? How was he tortured?

7. How did John get out of prison?

8. What are the major literary works of Saint John of the Cross?

9. Which spiritual writers were greatly influenced by the works of Saint John of the Cross?

10. What were the main attributes of Saint John's character?

TIME LINE OF THE AUTHOR'S LIFE

1. What does the name of Saint John of the Cross mean?

2. When was he born?

3. How old was John when he became a Roman Catholic priest?

4. When did Saint John of the Cross die?

THE CARMELITES

1. Where and when did the Carmelite Order begin?

2. How are the Carmelites organized?

3. Where is Mount Carmel?

4. How do the "calced" Carmelites and the "discalced" Carmelites differ from each other?

5. Which famous writers, monks, and other religious were members of the Carmelite Order?

SAINT TERESA OF AVILA—
CO-LABORER WITH JOHN OF THE CROSS

1. Who kept Teresa from becoming a Christian martyr? Under what circumstances might her martyrdom as a young child have occurred?

2. When and how did Teresa's experience as a mystic begin?

3. What steps did Teresa take in order to bring reform to the Carmelites?

4. What literary works is she most famous for?

5. According to Saint Teresa, what are the four stages in which the soul ascends to God?

"LOVE'S LIVING FLAME"

1. What do you see as the central theme of this poem?

2. How does God's love wound the soul?

3. What metaphors and similes are employed by the poet to make his points more vivid?

4. Is there any part of this poem or its commentary that you find disturbing? Why?

5. How does God change death into life for the soul?

6. Do you like this poem and its commentary? Why or why not?

THE SONG OF SOLOMON— KEY VERSES AND INSIGHTS

1. Who is the bride and who is the Bridegroom?

2. Which verse is the key verse of this chapter from the Bible, as it relates to the writings of Saint John of the Cross?

3. What are some other names for the Song of Solomon?

4. How are the bride and the Bridegroom described in the Song of Solomon?

5. Do you find the imagery that is employed by Solomon to be effective and vivid? Why or why not?

6. How does Saint John of the Cross relate the Song of Solomon to his writings?

THE SEVEN DEADLY SINS AND THE SEVEN HOLY VIRTUES

1. What are the Seven Deadly Sins? What do they all have in common?

2. What are the Seven Holy Virtues? What do they all have in common?

3. Which of the Seven Deadly Sins is the worst one? Why?

4. How does Saint John of the Cross use the Seven Deadly Sins and the Seven Holy Virtues in *Dark Night of the Soul*?

DARK NIGHT OF THE SOUL

1. What are the signs that show that a spiritual person is walking steadily along the way of the dark night?

2. What spiritual imperfections plague beginners most?

3. What benefits are caused within the soul as a result of its "dark night"?

4. Compare and contrast the "dark night of the soul" with the "dark night of the spirit."

5. What kinds of pain does the soul suffer during the "dark night of the spirit"?

6. How does the soul manage to walk securely even though it's in darkness?

7. Why does the devil have no access to the soul's hiding place?

8. What are the Ten Steps of the Mystic Ladder of Divine Love?

9. What is the role of divine wisdom as the soul continues its journey?

10. What is the soul's ultimate destiny in *Dark Night of the Soul*?

WORDS OF GOOD COUNSEL FROM SAINT JOHN OF THE CROSS

1. Select three of his quotes and tell what they mean to you.

2. What are four main subjects covered by Saint John of the Cross in these quotes?

BIBLIOGRAPHY

E. Allison Peers. *Saint John of the Cross, Living Flame of Love.* Burns and Oates, Tunbridge Wells, Kent, United Kingdom, 1977.

E. Allison Peers, *The Dark Night of the Soul* by John of the Cross. Image Books, 1959.

E. Allison Peers, *The Complete Works of Saint John of the Cross*, The Newman Bookshop, Westminster, MD, 1946.

Thomas S. Kepler, *The Fellowship of the Saints*, Abingdon-Cokesbury Press, Nashville, TN, 1948.

Kieran Kavanaugh, OCD and Otilio Rodriguez, OCD, *The Collected Works of St. John of the Cross*, ICS Publications, Washington, DC, 1979.

David Lewis, *A Spiritual Canticle of the Soul and the Bridegroom of Christ* by St. John of the Cross, June 28, 1909.

INDEX

Refreshing 210
rest xi, 13, 47, 55, 58, 78, 83, 84, 92, 93, 118, 135, 136,
151, 177, 178, 186, 199, 200, 202, 206, 245, 246,
247, 252, 253
Roman Catholic Church 5, 35, 45, 50, 67, 257, 258, 260,
262

S

safety 14, 252
Saint Augustine x, 127, 223
Saint Bernard viii, x, 220
Saint Bernard of Clairvaux x
Saint Ignatius Loyola 5
Saint Teresa Benedicta of the Cross 24
Saint Thomas viii, 24, 212, 220
Saint Thomas Aquinas 24
Salvation 176, 232
satan 126, 136, 241, 262
secret place 209
senses 19, 51, 78, 94, 102, 104, 107, 108, 109, 112, 113,
114, 115, 120, 121, 122, 123, 126, 127, 130, 134,
135, 136, 137, 138, 143, 144, 145, 146, 148, 149,
150, 159, 176, 184, 185, 193, 194, 210, 212, 213,
214, 215, 217, 233, 238, 239, 240, 247, 255, 259,
261, 262
sensuality 19, 97, 134, 135, 136, 151, 200, 201, 236
seraphim 263
service 4, 10, 39, 42, 84, 104, 164, 211, 224
sexual addiction 68
similes 53, 60, 268
sin 67, 68, 69, 70, 71, 72, 93, 96, 98, 99, 117, 128, 130,
131, 146, 221, 227, 254, 257, 259, 262
Sloth 71, 104
sodomy 68
Solomon xiii, 7, 18, 21, 22, 53, 55, 56, 57, 58, 59, 60,
61, 62, 63, 64, 65, 66, 113, 199, 212, 221, 224,
227, 233, 234, 235, 239, 240, 245, 248, 249, 268,

Pure Gold Classics

AN
EXPANDING
COLLECTION
OF THE
BEST-LOVED
CHRISTIAN
CLASSICS OF
ALL TIME.

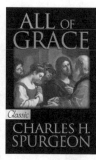

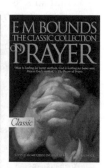

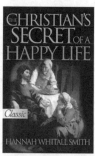

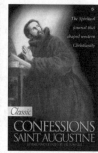

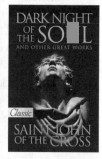

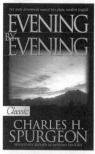

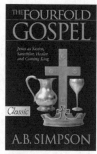

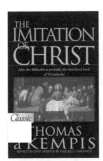
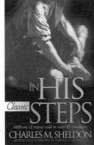

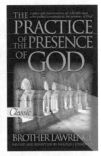
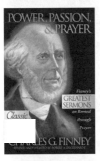

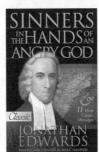
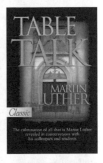
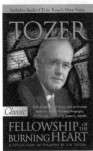
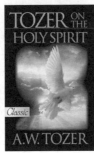
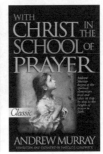
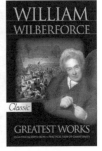

Pure Gold Classics

CHRISTIAN CLASSICS

A classic is a work of enduring excellence; a Christian classic is a work of enduring excellence that is filled with divine wisdom, biblical revelation, and insights that are relevant to living a godly life. Such works are both spiritual and practical. Our Pure Gold Classics contain some of the finest examples of Christian writing that have ever been published, including the works of John Foxe, Charles Spurgeon, D.L. Moody, Martin Luther, John Calvin, Saint John of the Cross, E.M. Bounds, John Wesley, Andrew Murray, Hannah Whitall Smith, and many others.

The timeline on the following pages will help you to understand the context of the times in which these extraordinary books were written and the historical events that must have served to influence these great writers to create works that will always stand the test of time. Inspired by God, many of these authors did their work in difficult times and during periods of history that were not sympathetic to their message. Some even had to endure great persecution, misunderstanding, imprisonment, and martyrdom as a direct result of their writing.

The entries that are printed in green type will give you a good overview of Christian history from the birth of Jesus to modern times.

The entries in red pertain to writers of Christian classics from Saint Augustine, who wrote his *Confessions* and *City of God*, to Charles Sheldon, twentieth-century author of *In His Steps*.

Entries in black provide a clear perspective on the development of secular history from the early days of Buddhism (first century) through the Civil Rights Movement.

Finally, the blue entries highlight secular writers and artists, including Chaucer, Michelangelo, and others.

Our color timeline will provide you with a fresh perspective of history, both secular and Christian, and the classics, both secular and Christian. This perspective will help you to understand each author better and to see the world through his or her eyes.